spatial configuration

99.01
99.03 Fenil
011 adidas WoS
03.08 Theater Stadthof
03.10 Wohnungen
04.02 International
Nanjing
04.03 adidas football
04.05 ZIS Zurich
04.06 Einhausung
04.09 Polizei- und
05.01 Wolfratshausen
05.06 Papierfabrik
05.13 adidas
05.14 Uni Darmstadt
06.01 Integra H2 H4
06.01 Integra i37
06.04 München
09.25 Gornergrat
10.07 Integra
11.08 ZHAW Campus
09.02 adidas Baufeld
11.18 Aedes Berlin
12.09 Wallisellen
12.15 Im Glattgarten
12.16 Esslingen
13.03 Zahnradfabrik
13.04 Studien Brig Glis
13.06 Zollstrasse
13.07 la galerie
16.04 Hochschulcampus
16.06 Regierungsviertel
16.08 Röntgenhof
16.09 Schulhaus
16.11 Gemeindehaus
16.12 EKZ
16.13 Riverside Zuchwil
16.14 Russenweg
16.15 New Cyprus
16.16 Kantonsschule
17.01 Stadtarchiv und
17.03
17.10 Esslinger Dreieck

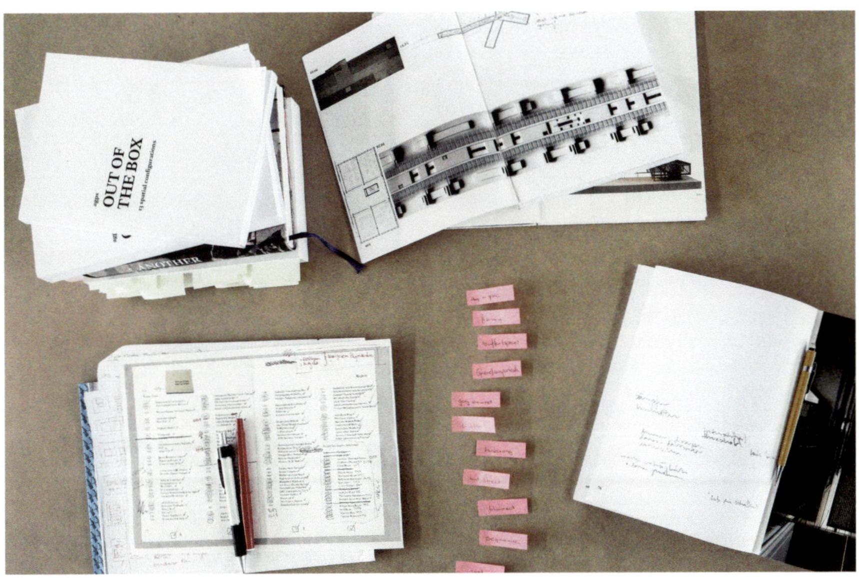
OUT OF
THE BOX

agps Manuel Scholl, Marc Angélil, Sarah Graham

agps

OUT OF THE BOX

13 Spatial Configurations

Park Books

Object in Space

Object in Space

0907

Object in Space

0215

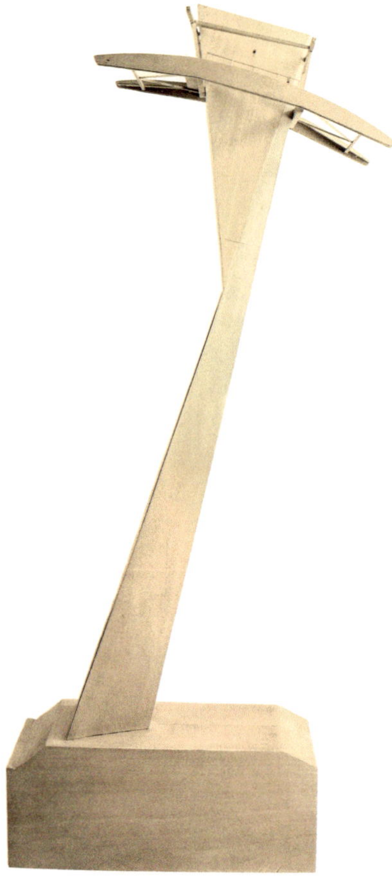

Object in Space

Object in Space

0313

1615

Object in Space

9901

Object in Space

1810

1415

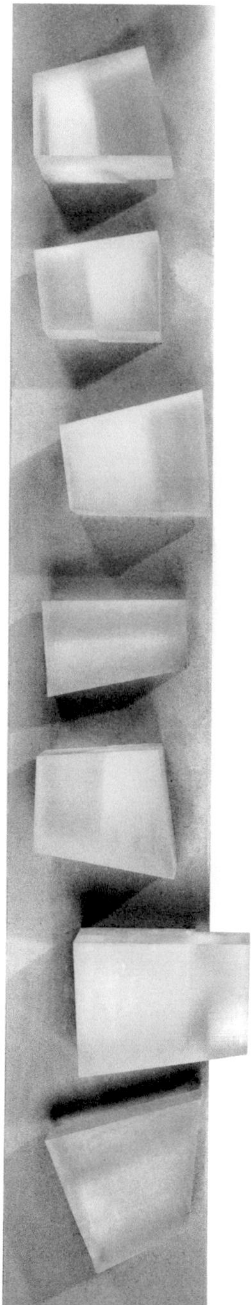

0409

Object in Space

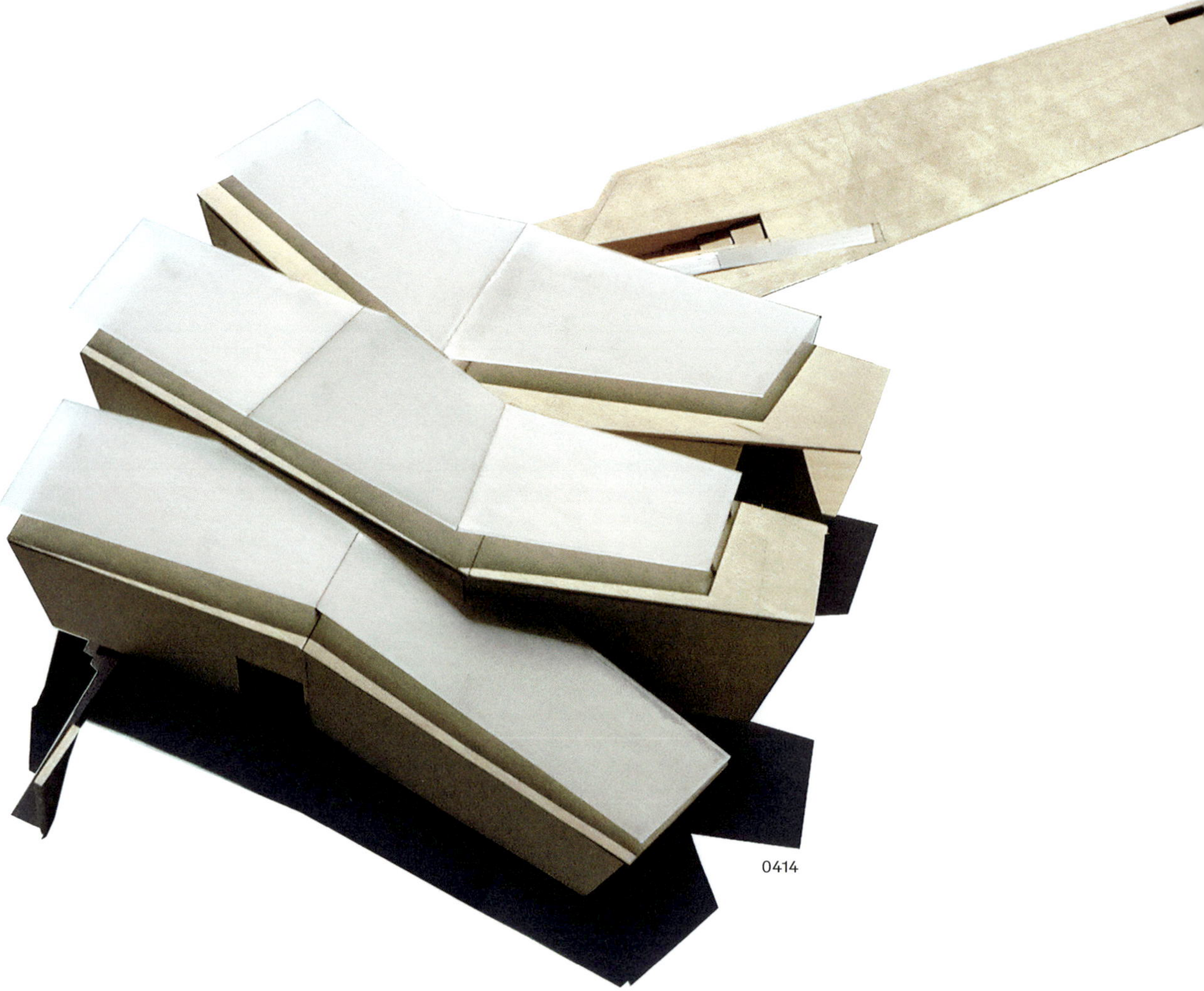

0414

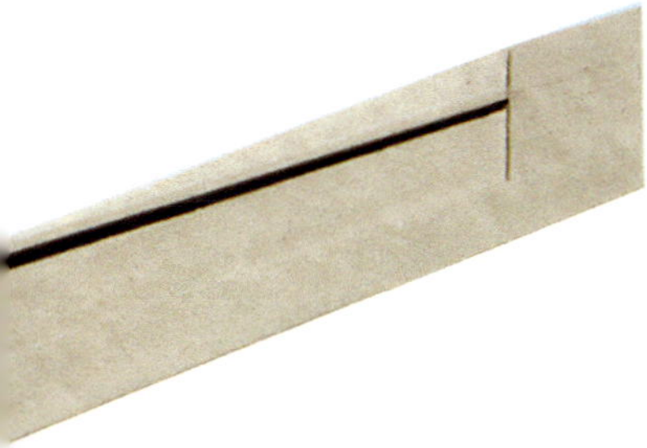

Object in Space

Object in Space

0303

Object in Space

Framing

9102

Framing

0925

9801

Framing

0514

1215

Framing

9102

0414

Framing

1613

0814

Framing

0814

0907

Framing

0302

1306

Framing

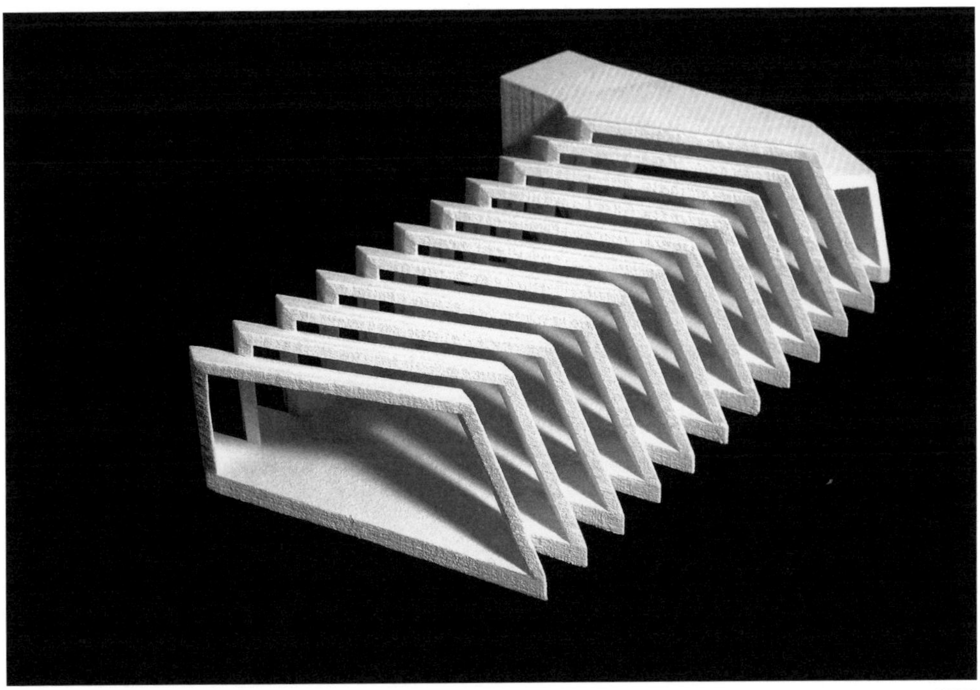

0302

Buffer

Buffer

Buffer

Buffer

9701

Buffer

0601

Buffer

9206

Conglomerate

Conglomerate

Conglomerate

0628

Conglomerate

Conglomerate

0308

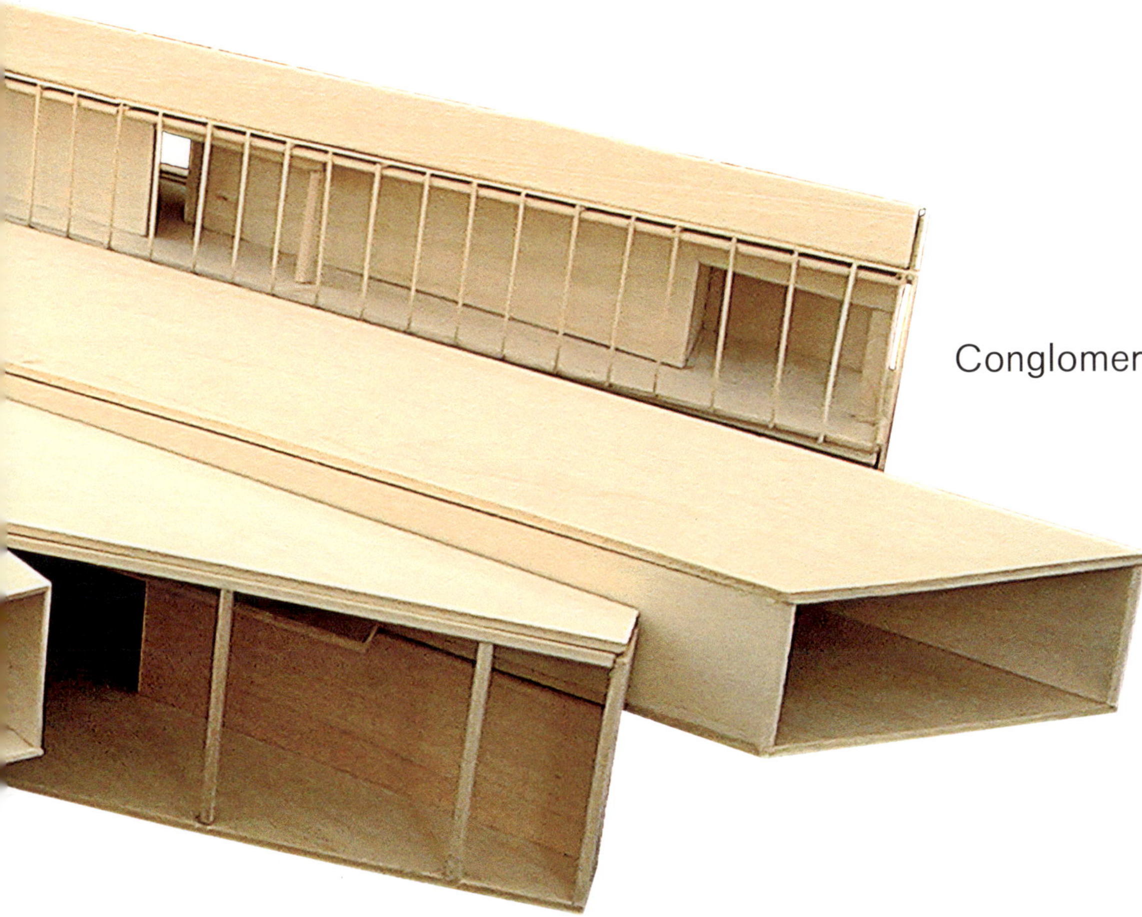

Conglomerate

Conglomerate

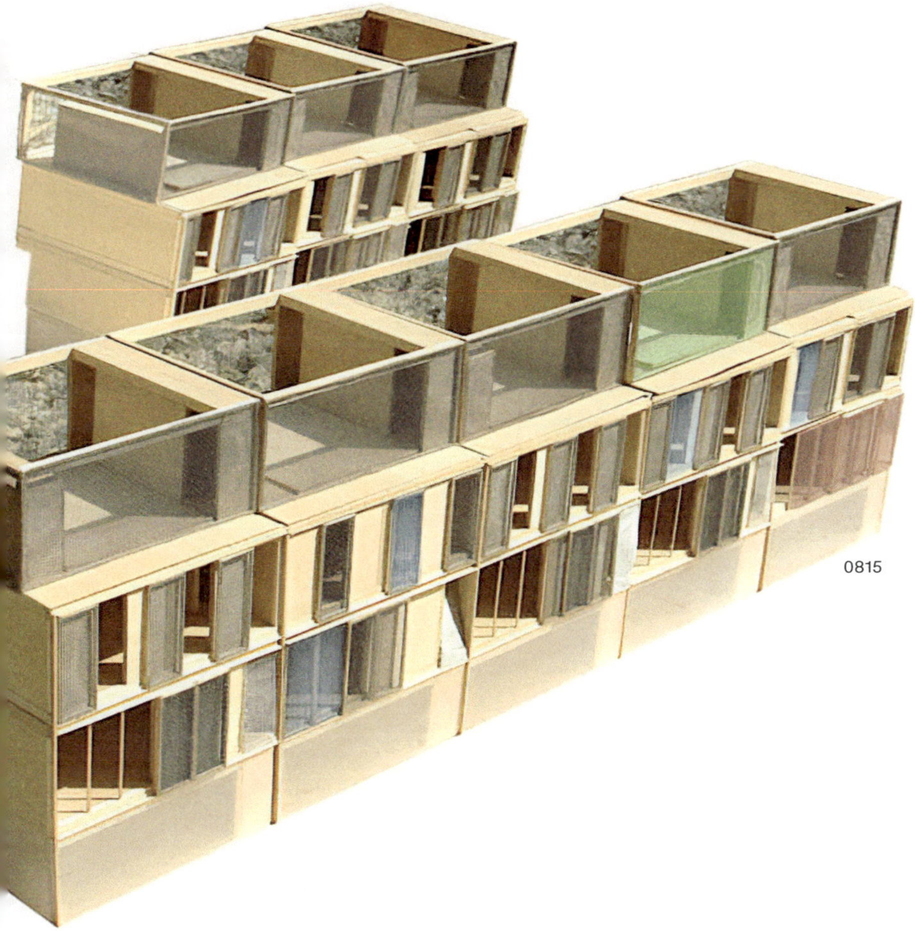

0815

Conglomerate

1611

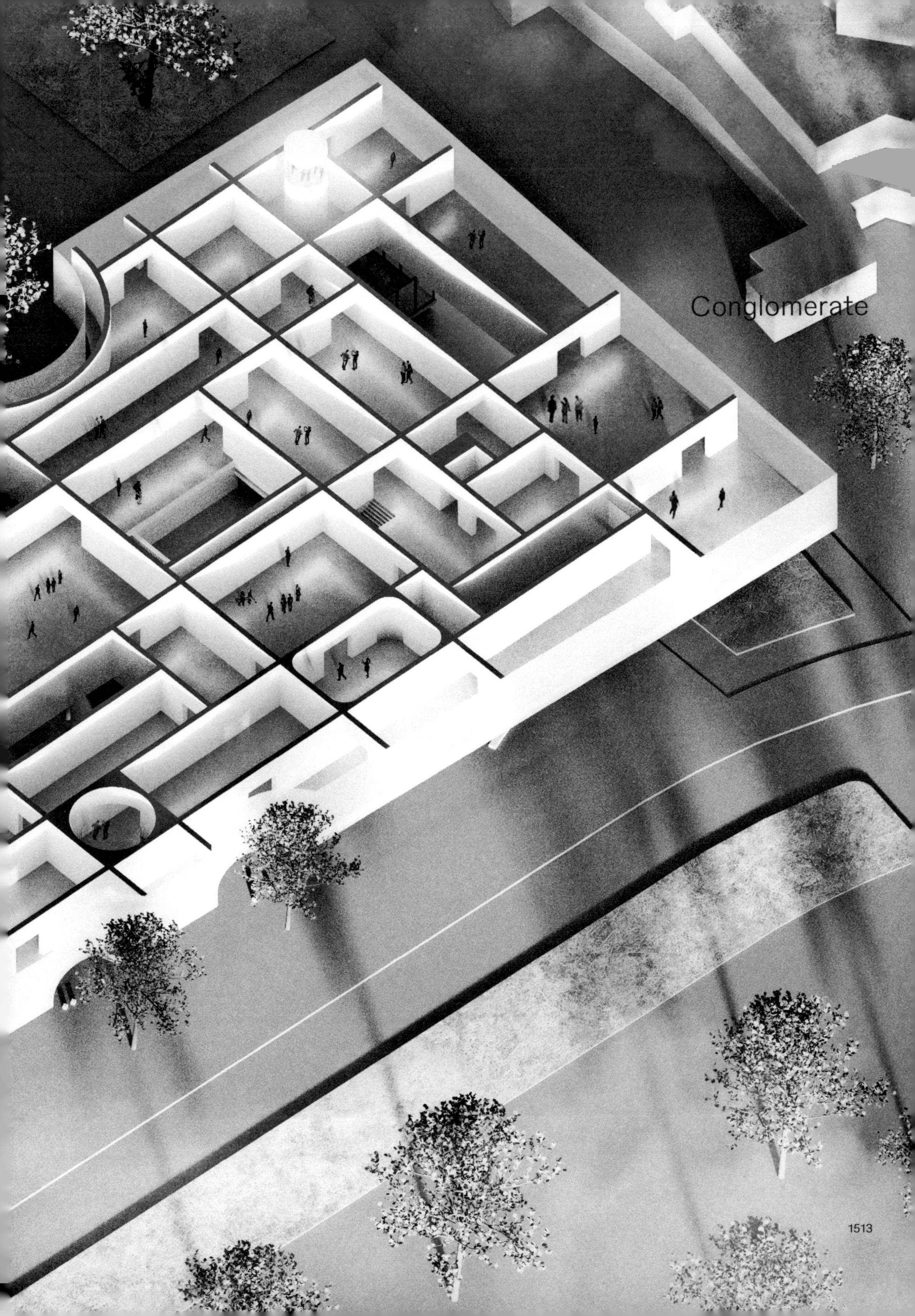
Conglomerate

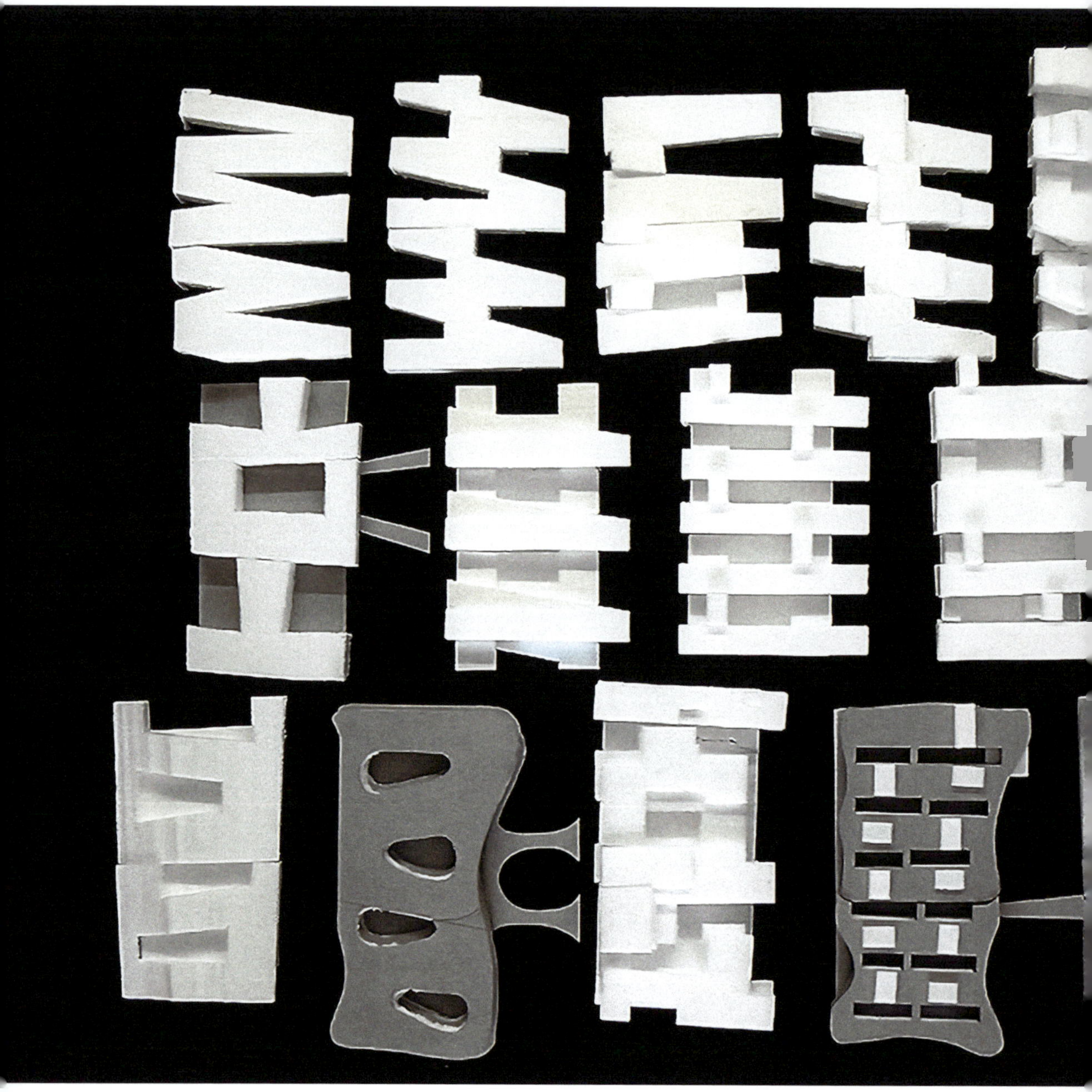

Conglomerate

Conglomerate

9402

Conglomerate

Linear

Linear

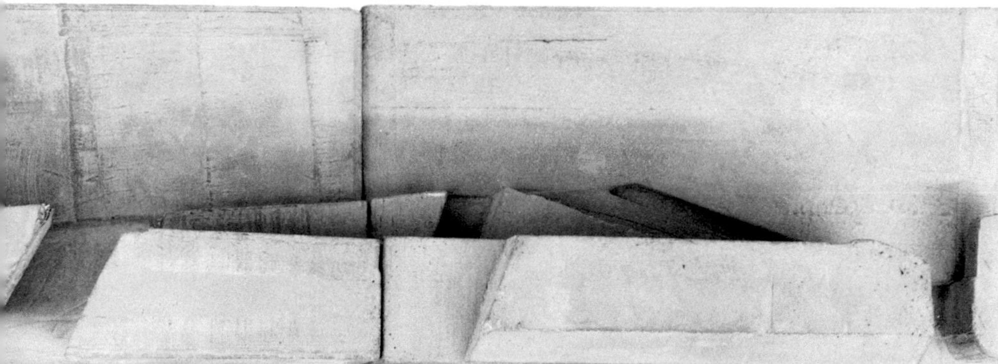

1306

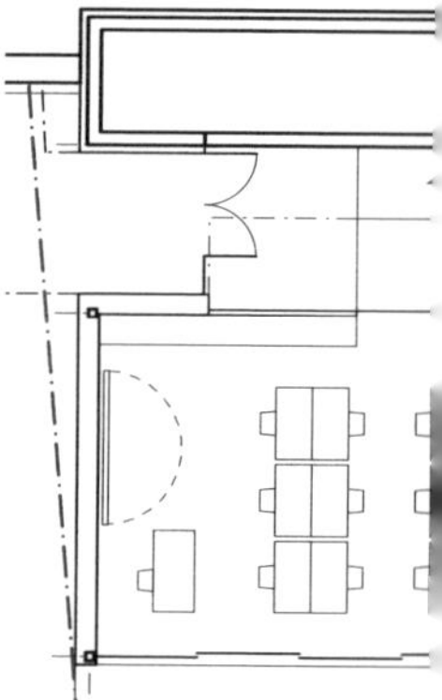

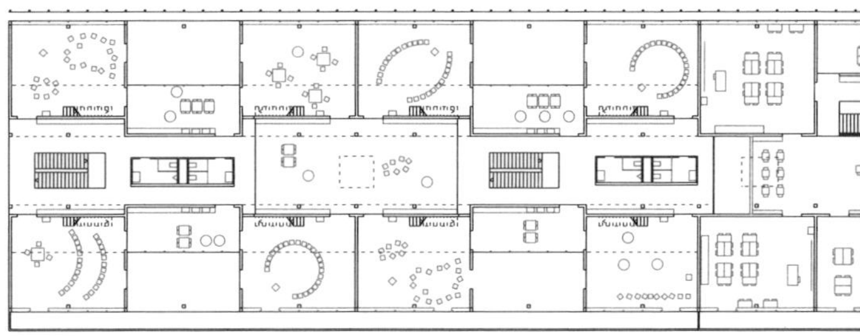

Linear

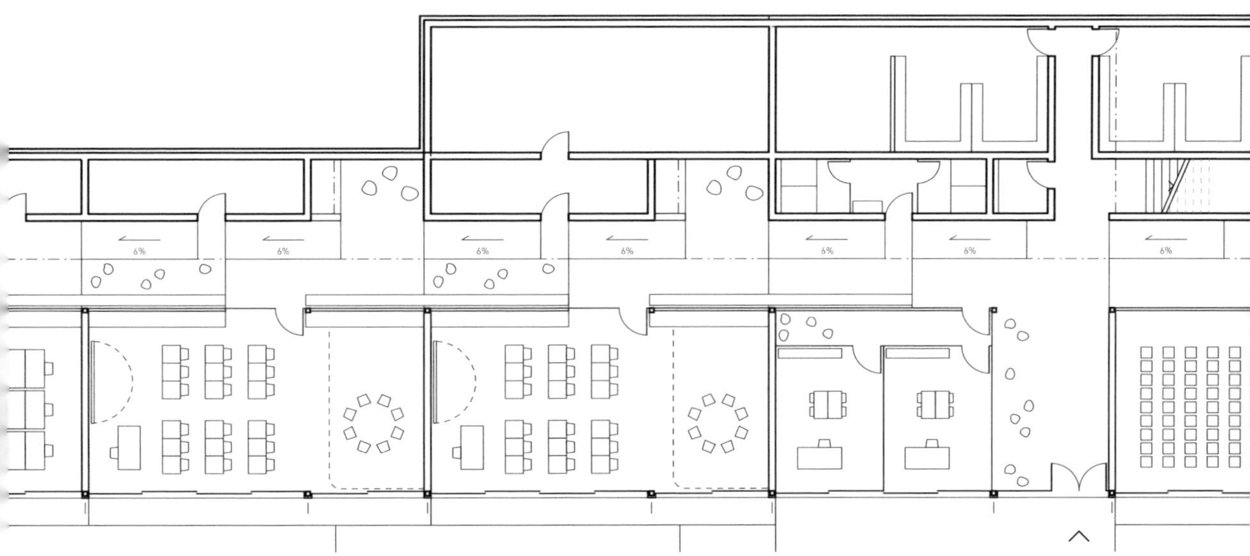

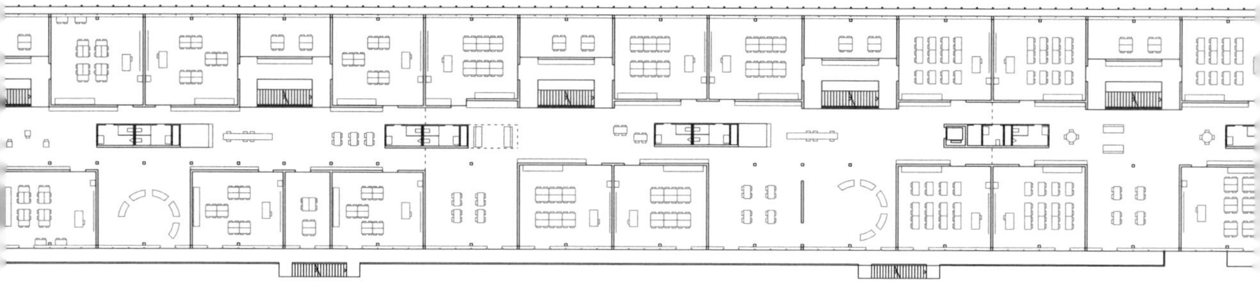

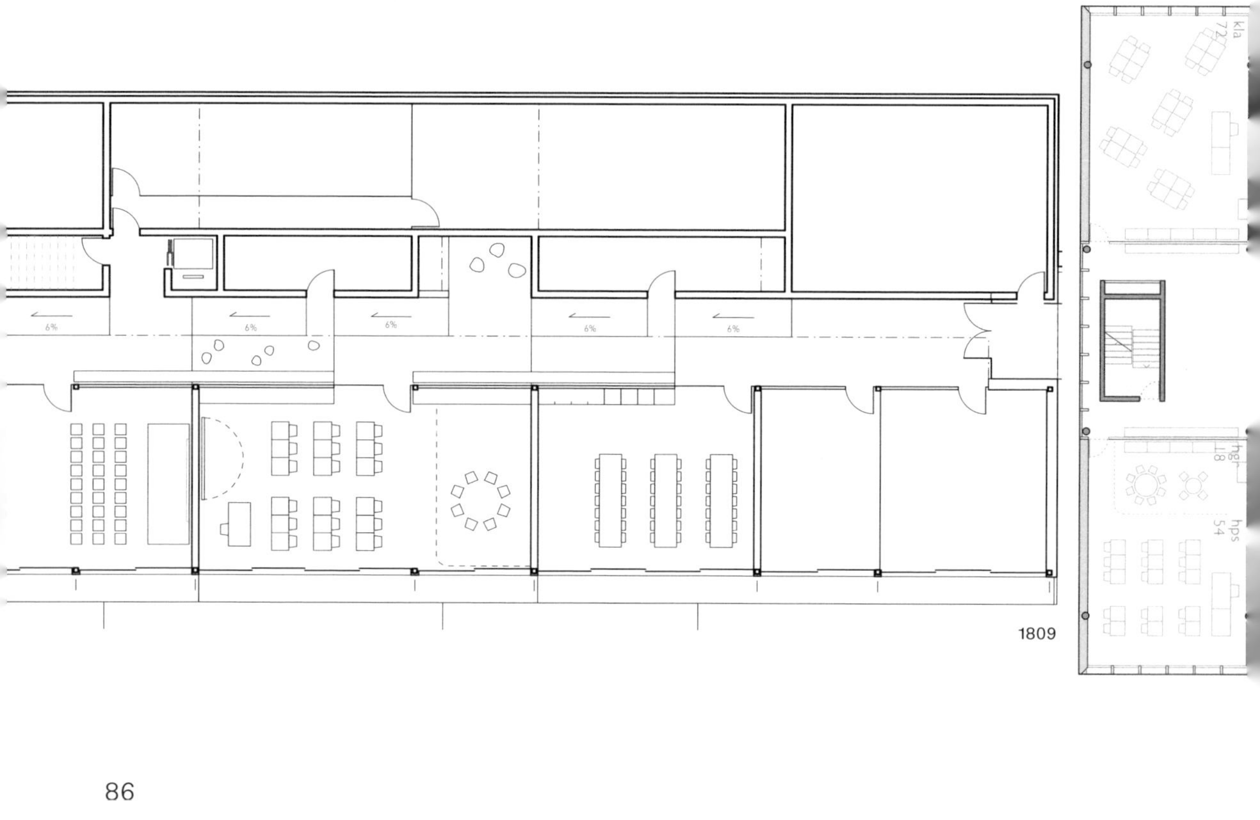

1809

0908

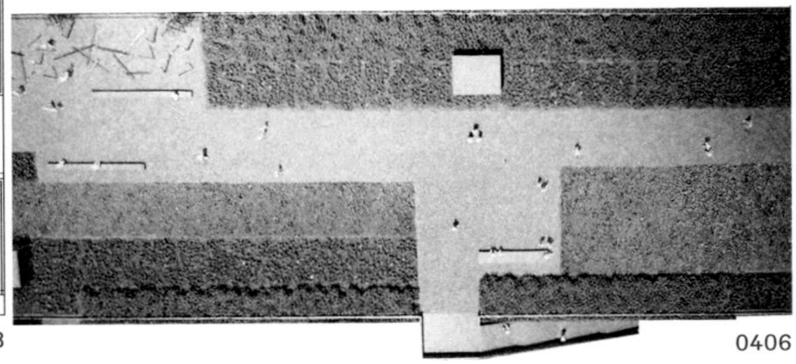

0406

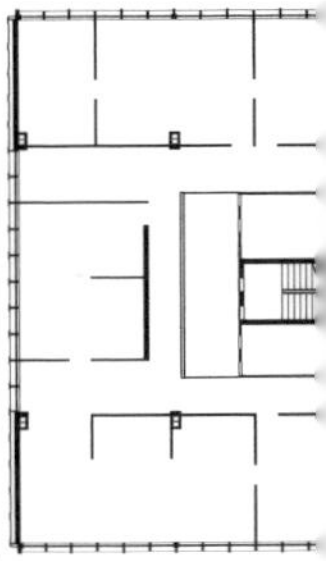

Linear

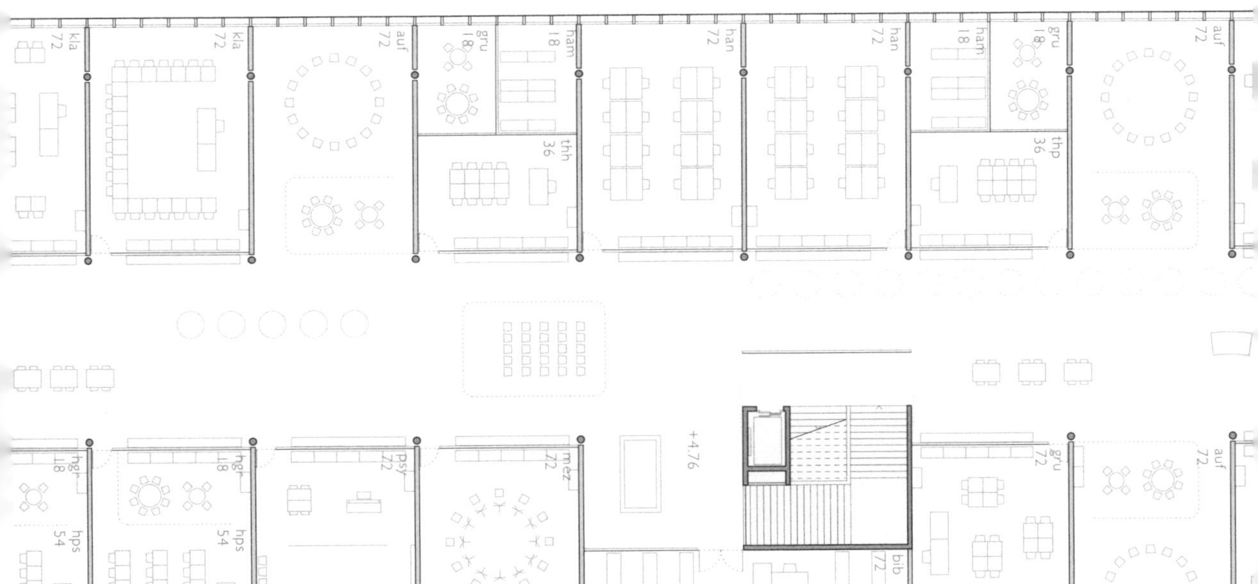

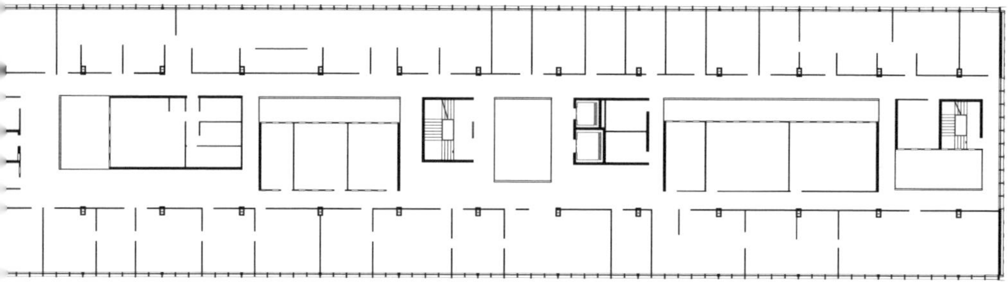

1414

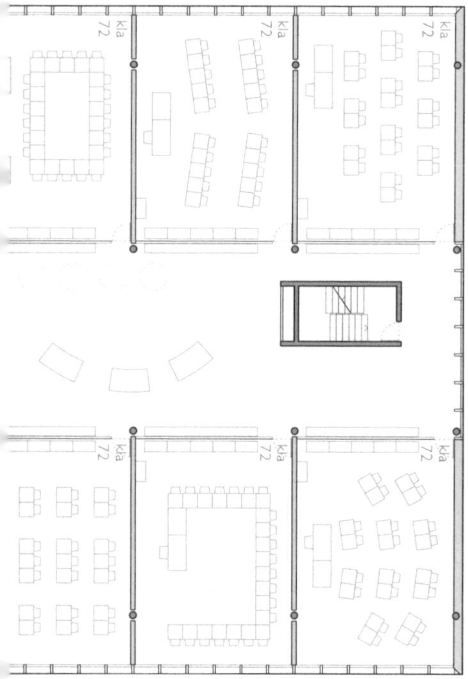

1609

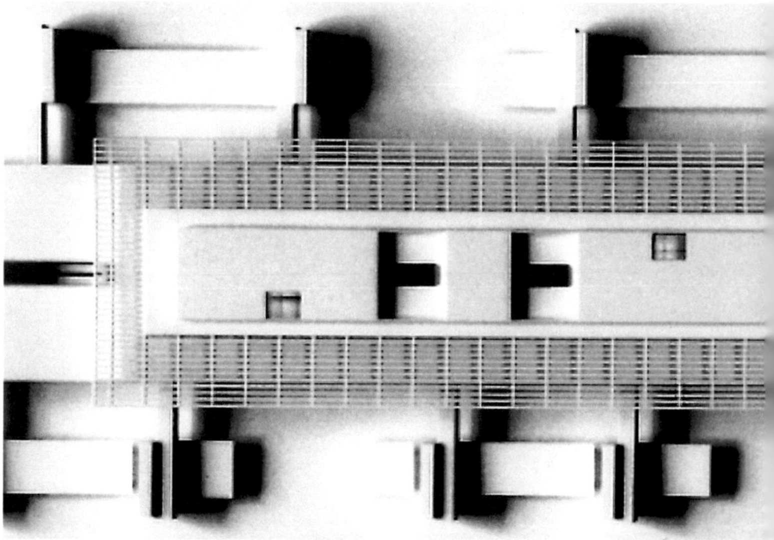

0405

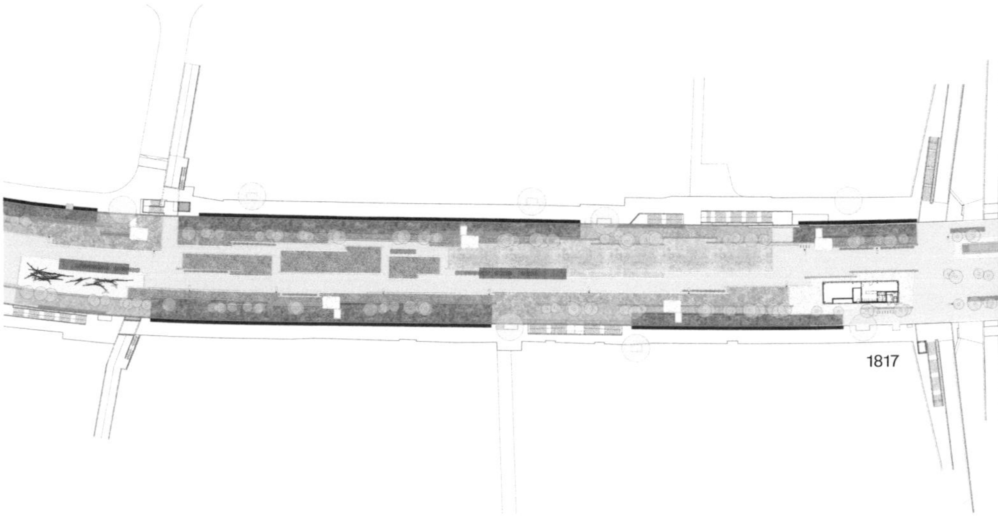

1817

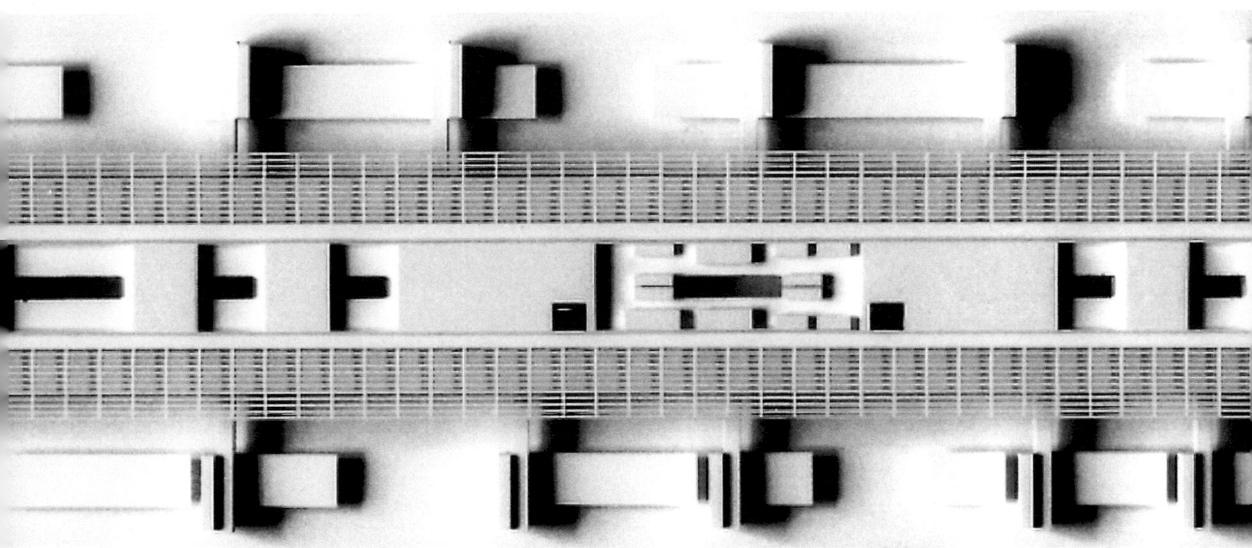

0406

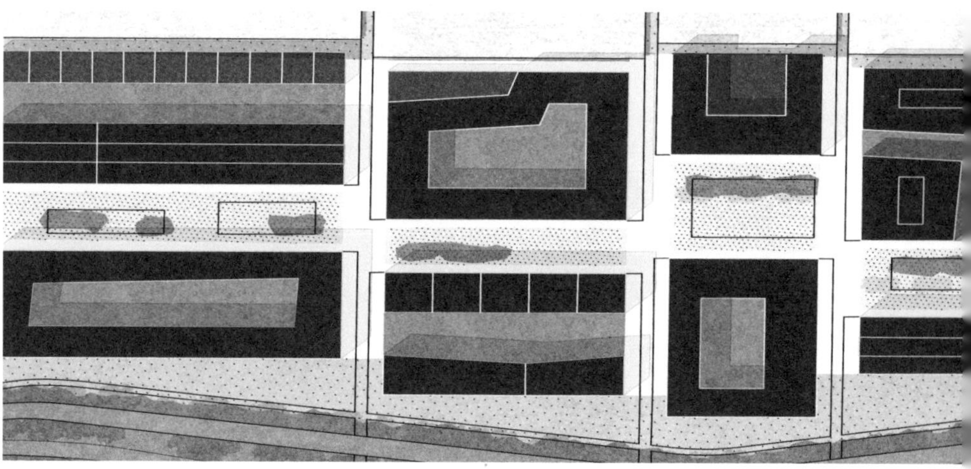

9701

0605

1116

Linear

1805

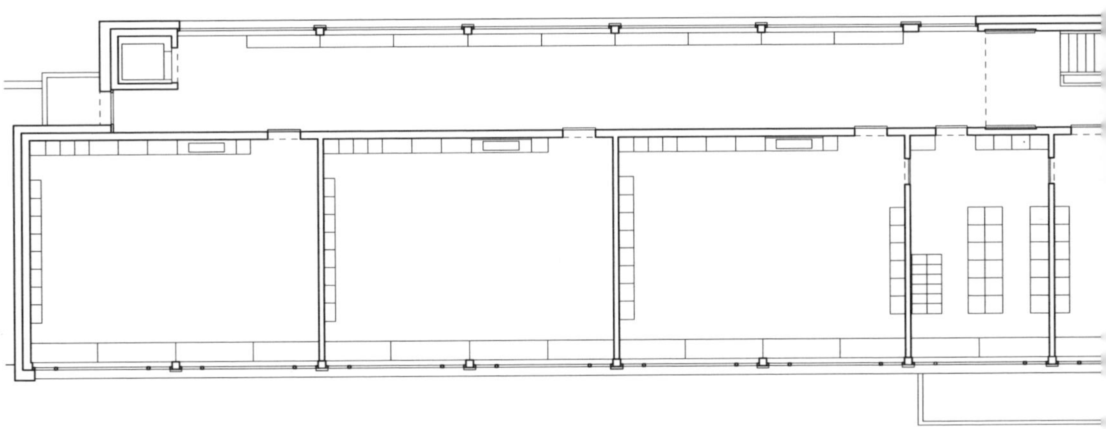

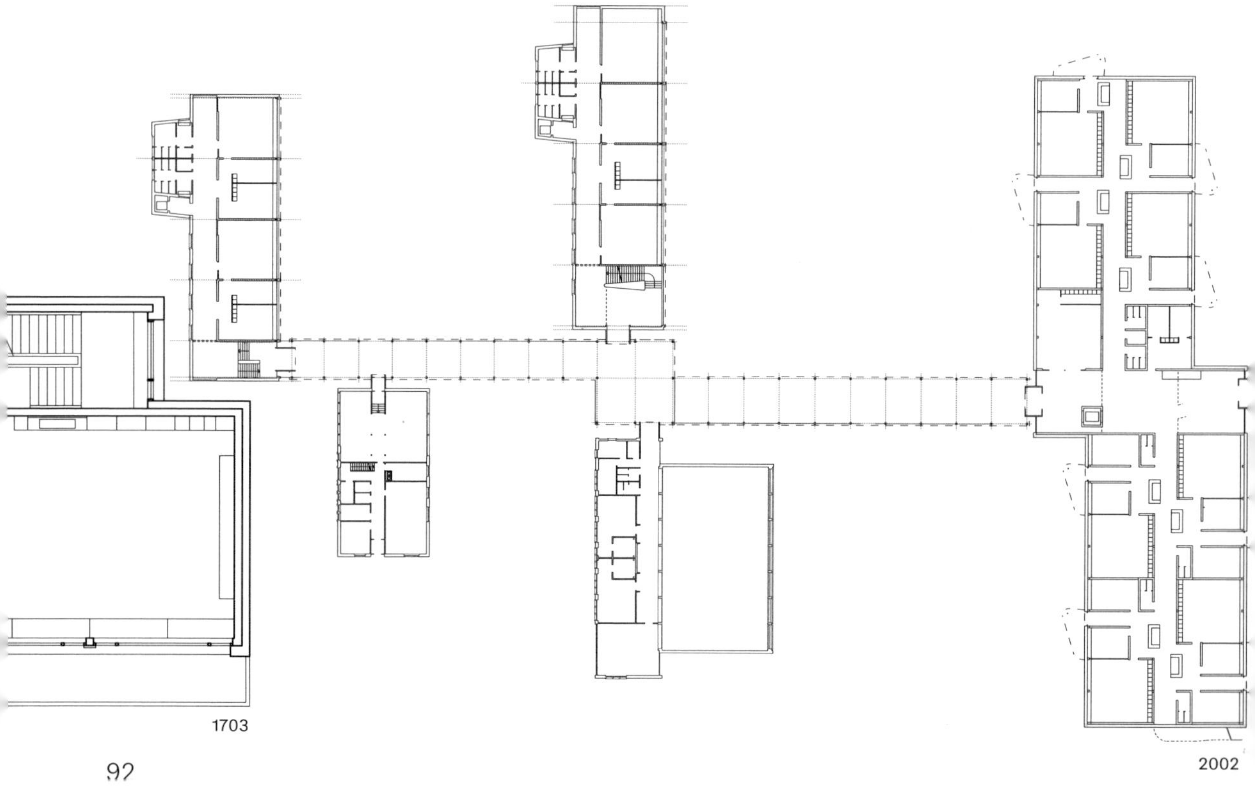
1703
2002

Linear

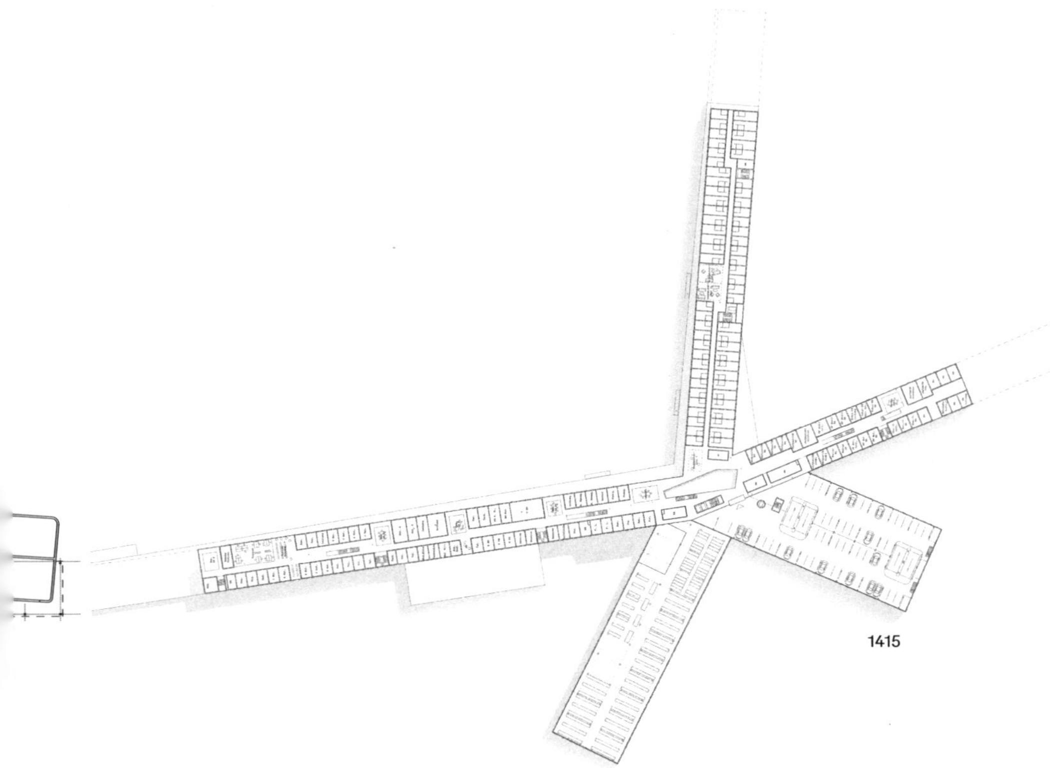

1415

Under the Roof

Under the Roof

1108

Under the Roof
9701

Under the Roof

1617

9204

Under the Roof
9103

9701

Under the Roof

9202

Under the Roof

9903

Under the Roof

9102

Under the Roof

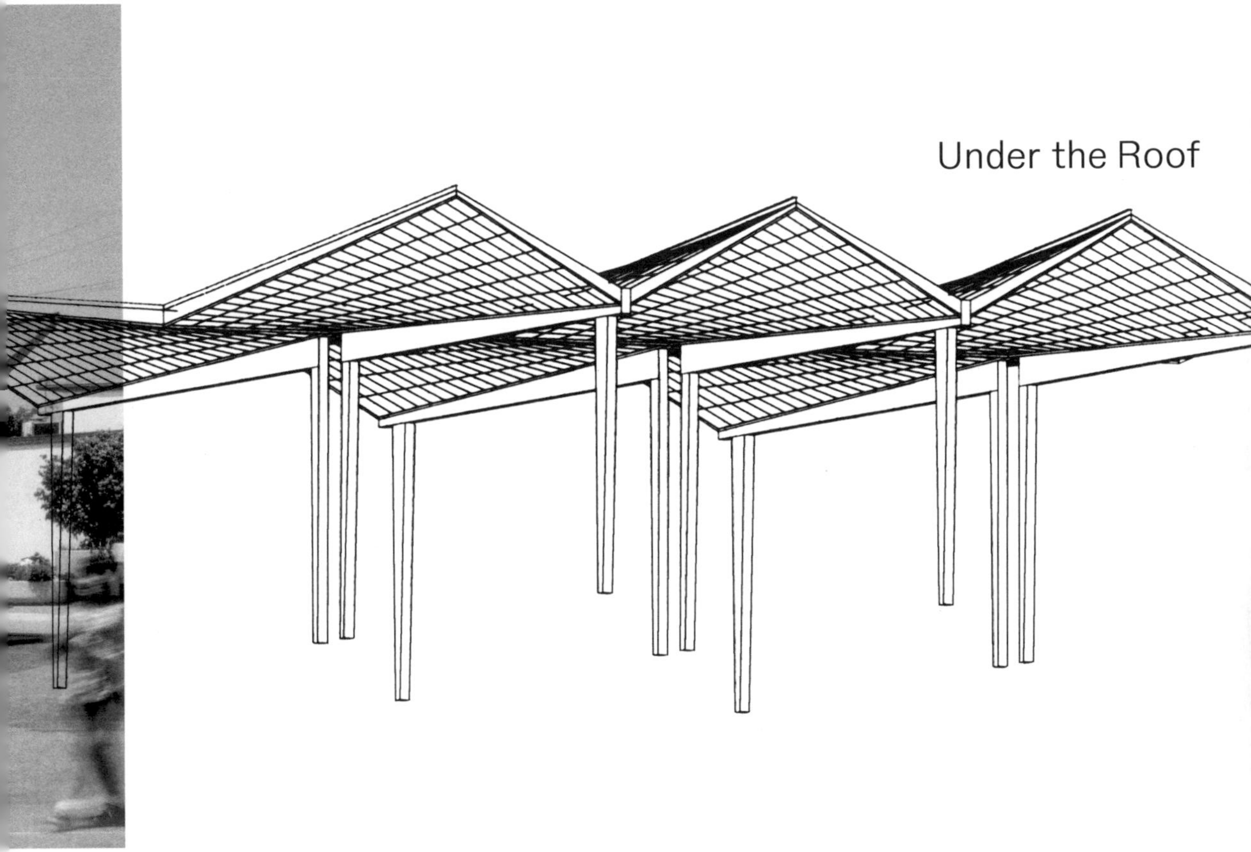

9001

9505

Under the Roof

Going Around

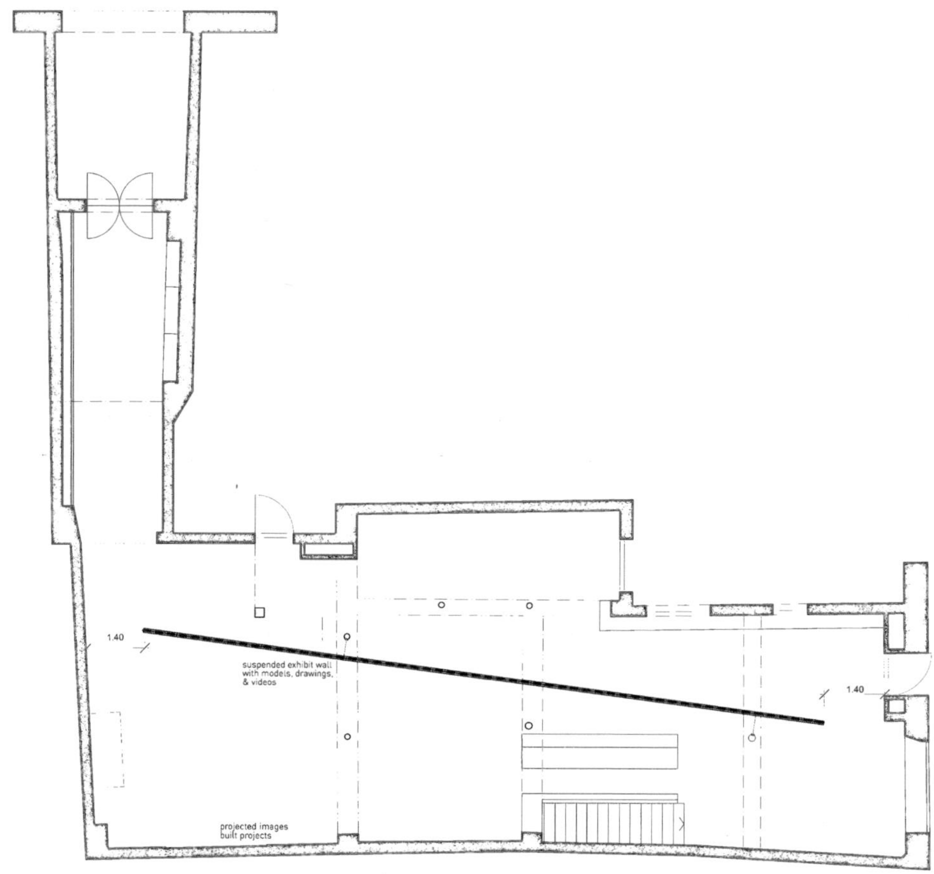
1.40
suspended exhibit wall
with models, drawings,
& videos
1.40
projected images
built projects

1307

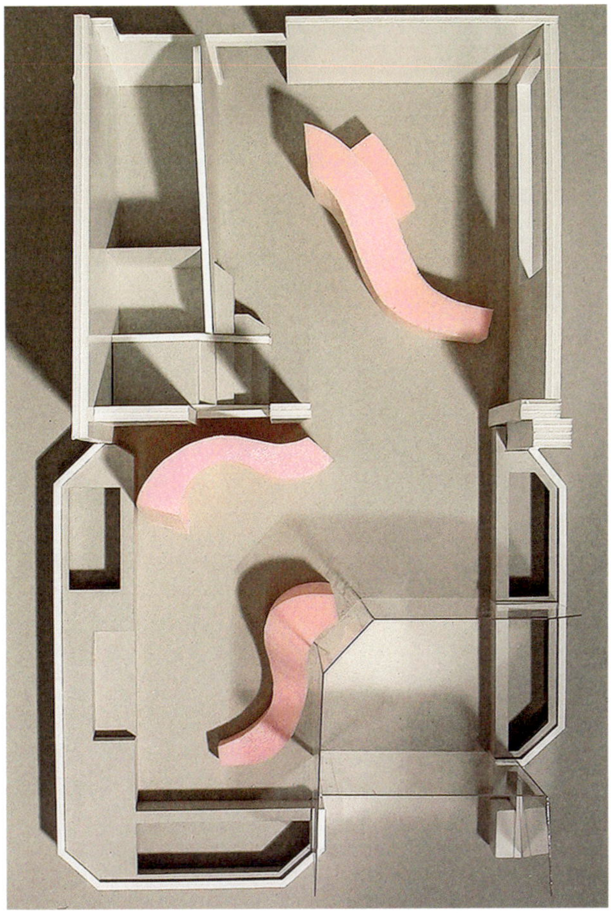

0611

Going Around

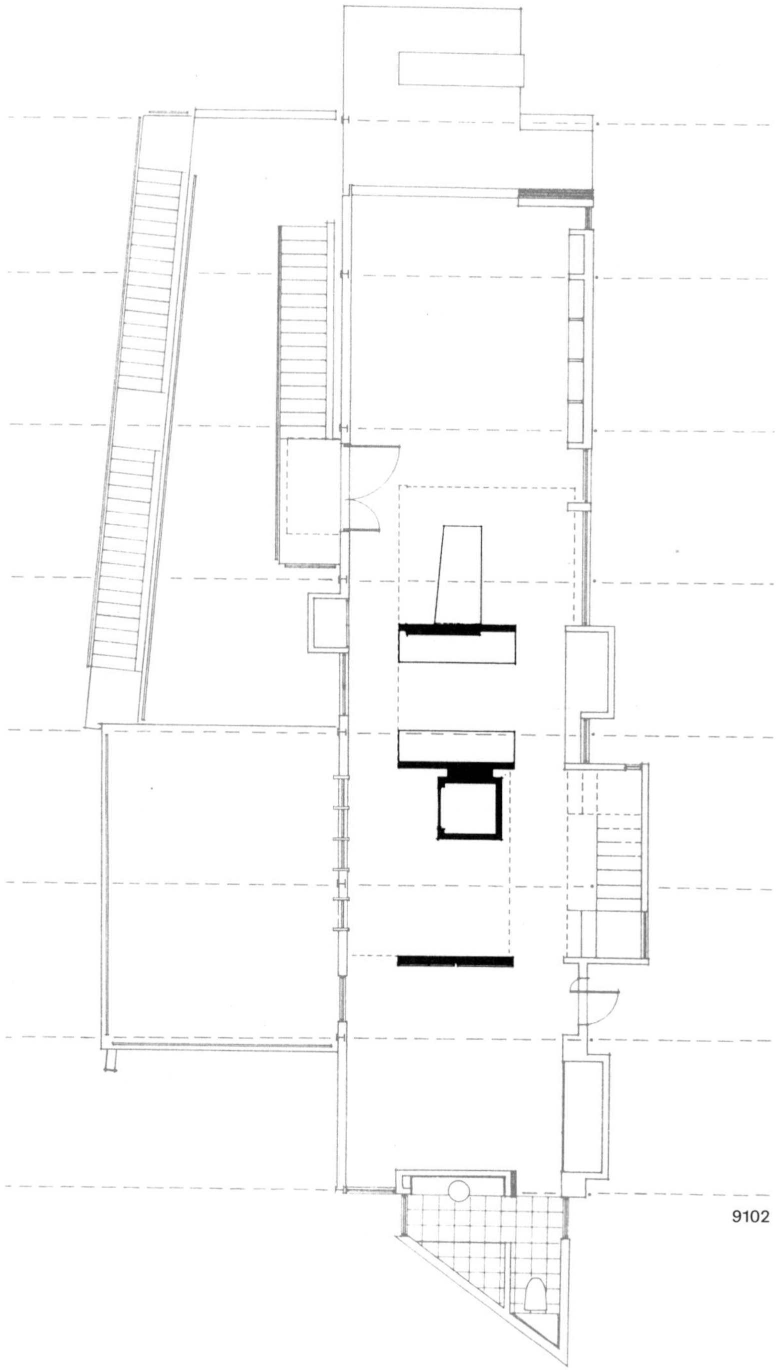

9102

1614

Going Around

0101

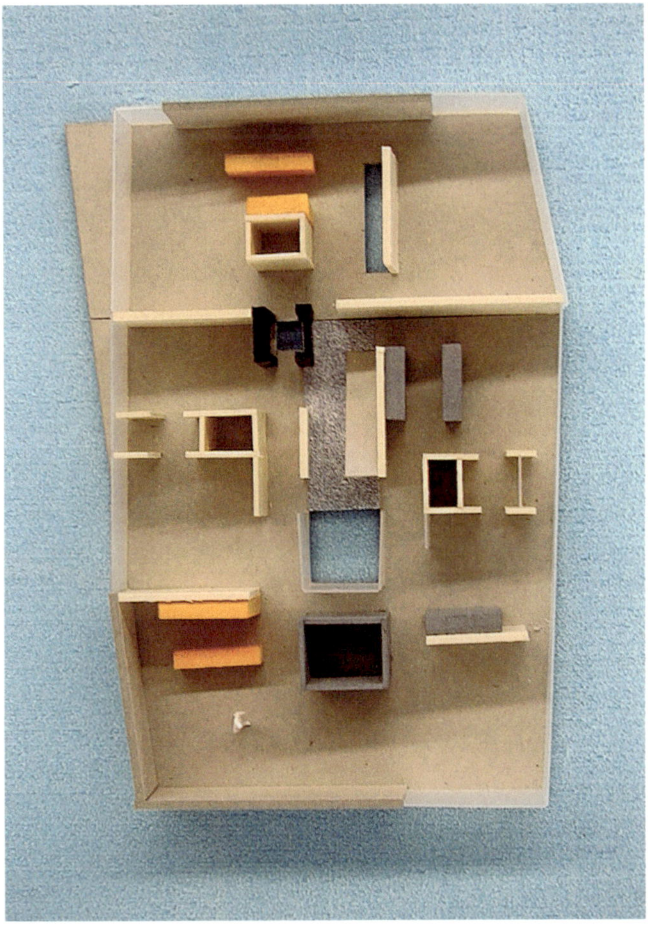

Going Around

0301

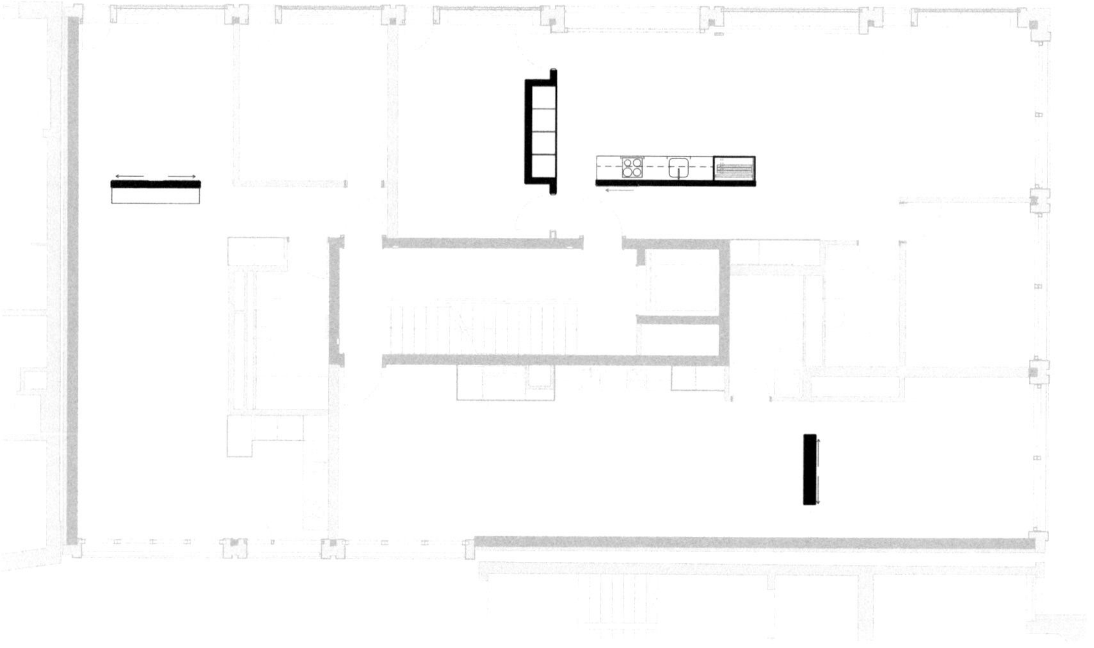

1803

Going Around

1711

Going Around

1902

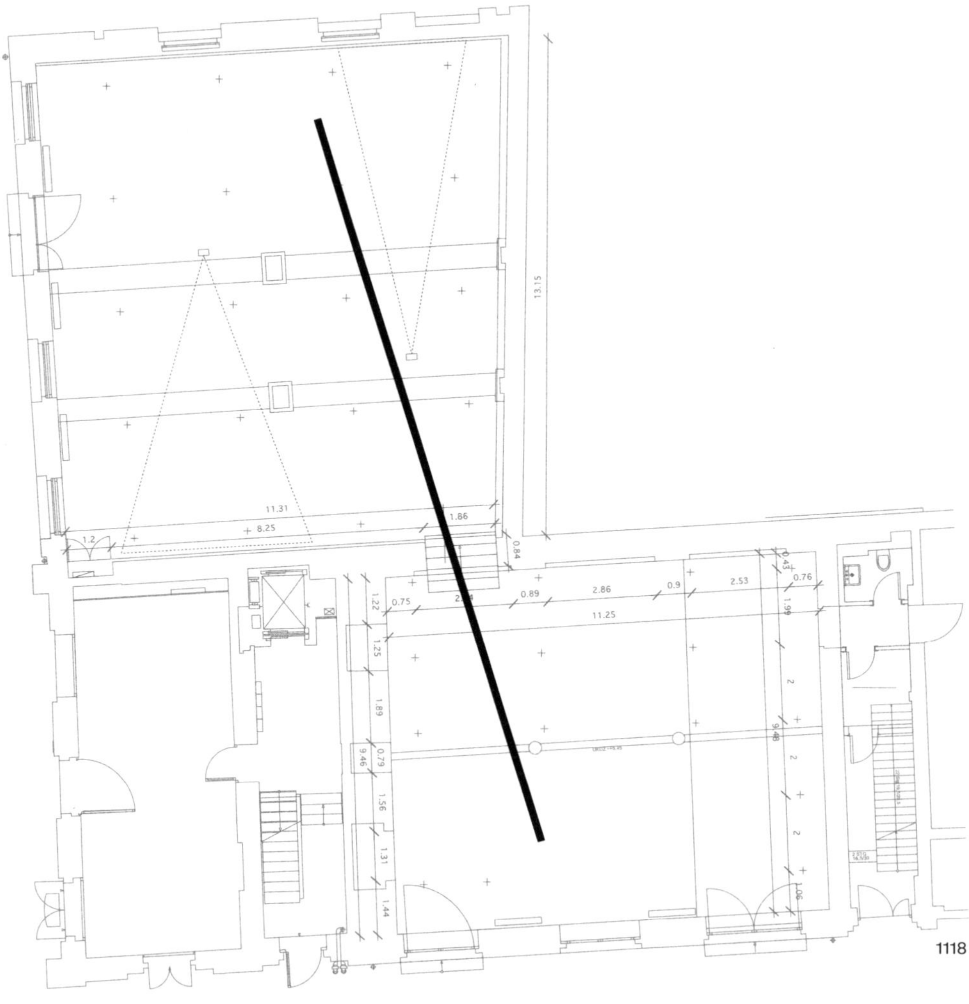
11.31
1.86
1.2
8.25
0.84
13.15
0.75
0.89
2.86
0.9
2.53
0.76
11.25
1.22
1.25
1.89
9.46
0.79
1.56
1.31
1.44
1.99
2
2
2
1.06

1118

Going Around

1118

Hidden

0301

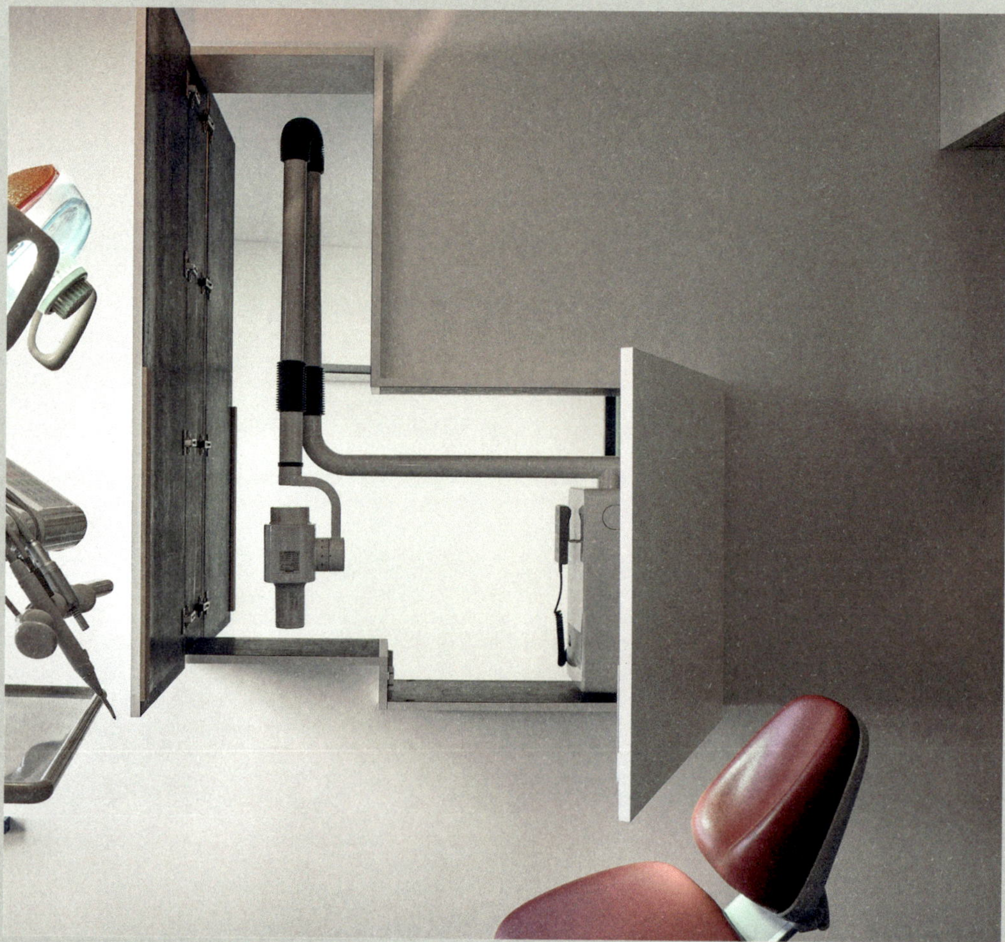
9403

Hidden

0411

Hidden

Hidden
0406

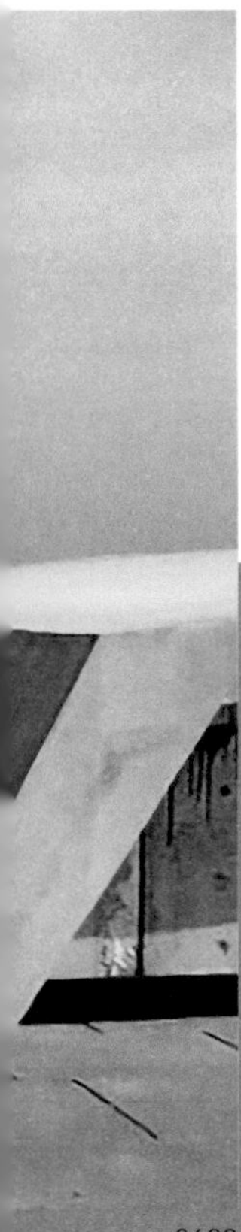

0403

Hidden

Hidden

1615

Hidden

1510

Sabine von Fischer – Pensée Sauvage

Gedanken einfangen

Manchmal notieren wir die Gedanken, um sie einzufangen. Nur eine konkrete Logik wird dem wilden Denken gerecht – so zumindest empfahl es der Neuerfinder der Ethnologie Claude Lévi-Strauss im Jahr 1962. An Konkretem fehlt es der Architektur nicht: Jeder Strich, jedes Wort, jede Oberfläche bezieht sich auf ein konkretes Objekt. Architekt*innen denken an Schraubenköpfe und Regionalpläne, an Kunst und Technik, Wissenschaft und Alltag. Es gibt mehrfache Verbindungen zwischen diesen Bereichen, zuweilen erscheinen sie zahllos.

Out of the box

agps sind viele, und sie sind überall. Wer sie in Zürich sucht, wird mit Los Angeles verbunden, auch mit Santa Ynez oder Barcelona. Sie sind auch in Gedanken an vielen Orten. «Out of the box» auf dem Umschlag ihres kaleidoskopischen Bilderbuchs spielt auf wörtliche und übertragene Bedeutungen an: Die Box ist das Archiv, in dem Modelle, Zeichnungen und Daten vor Staub und Cyberattacken geschützt sind. Die Box steht aber auch für die Norm, aus der sich die Architekt*innen immer wieder befreit haben.

Drehbuch

Eigentlich platzt diese Box aus allen Nähten: Das Material ist kantig, flüchtig, zu gross, zu sperrig, ufert aus, zerfliesst. Es lässt sich kaum komprimieren. Trotzdem haben wir, als ich in den 1990er-Jahren Praktikantin bei agps war, den Versuch einer Ordnung unternommen. Auf hunderten von kleinen Blättern haben wir das Drehbuch ihrer ersten Zürcher Büropräsentationen notiert, vor fast dreissig Jahren in Fritz Schwarz' Kellertheater, dem Architekturforum am Neumarkt.

Einladungen

«Offene Strukturen» titelten die sechs Architekt*innen von agps damals. Später hiessen ihre Werkvorträge oft wie die Projekte: einfach und konkret. Die Offenheit im Denken und die Freiheit zu assoziieren trat immer wieder an die Oberfläche. Bei Einladungen zu Vorträgen sprachen sie über «Heterogene Produktionen» und über «Topolektisches Zeichnen», im Lauf der Jahrzehnte auch über Tango, Wurzelnetze, Cadavres Exquis, Utopien und Millennium Models.

Unschärfe

Wir hatten keinen Vortrag, sondern ein Filmskript geschrieben. Mit diesem Format wollten wir uns die Freiheit, assoziativ und wild zu denken, offenhalten. Es waren mehr als zweihundert Kärtchen, mehr als zweihundert Dias, und viel mehr als zweihundert Ideen, mit denen wir das Publikum auf den kühlen steinernen Stufen im Keller am Neumarkt dann verzaubert oder eher: überwältigt haben. Das Klicken ist mir noch im Ohr, dieser viel zu schnelle Rhythmus, der durch sein Tempo eine Unschärfe erzeugte und sich allen Regeln der Vortragskunst widersetzte.

Pensée Sauvage

Bewegung

Die Regeln allerdings interessierten uns brennend. Wir lasen Umberto Eco und dachten über das Chaos der Relationen nach, in dem sich neue Regeln bilden: vielleicht solche, die wir noch nicht kannten, Regeln in Bewegung für ein Kunstwerk in Bewegung. Dieses biete die Möglichkeit für eine Vielzahl persönlicher Eingriffe, lasen wir beim Papst der Semiotik, Umberto Eco (*Die Poetik des offenen Kunstwerks*, 1962).

Pensée Sauvage

Diese Texte aus den Jahren des intellektuellen Aufbruchs der Nachkriegszeit berührten uns. Wir orientierten uns am «wilden Denken» und assoziierten damit noch viel mehr, als Lévi-Strauss seinen Leser*innen vermutlich je zutraute. Wir falteten Dächer und knickten Fassaden und liessen die Topografie der Landschaft in den Häusern nachklingen.

Wildes Denken

Auf einem Buchumschlag von Lévi-Strauss (*La pensée sauvage*, 1962) ist eine *pensée* abgebildet (auch *fleur de pense* oder *viola tricolor*), ein wildes Stiefmütterchen. An ihr demonstriert er die These der konkreten Logik. Wie verschiedene ethnografische Texte bezeugen, sind an den Blütenblättern die Verwandtschaften zu den Eltern der Pflanze ablesbar: Wildes Denken und wilde Pflanzen organisieren sich nach bestimmten Regeln.

Schmerzen lindern

Wildnis verstehen: Das wilde Stiefmütterchen lindert Entzündungen und Schmerzen, die im Garten kultivierten Veilchensorten bleiben wirkungslos. Auch die Gedanken sollen wild, bewegt, offen, inspiriert, improvisiert bleiben und von überallher kommen.

Lesarten

Fliegen lassen, fassen, die Zwischenräume ausloten. Vielleicht sind sie längst verdichtet, amalgamiert, wer liest denn nicht zwischen den Zeilen? Jetzt, wo die Reihenfolge der Abbildungen gesetzt ist, wer darf jetzt noch spielen? Die Gedanken sind frei und verbinden sich mit anderen Bruchstücken. Verflechtungen verdichten sich zu Netzen.

Ein Rhizom

«Offene Strukturen», wie auch spätere Vorträge, Ausstellungen, Projekte, war ein Feuerwerk aus Bildern und Worten, Fragmente von Architekturideen, von denen viele nicht gebaut waren, sich vielmehr als Gedanken ihre Wege bahnten. Sie erschienen auf dem Papier von Wettbewerbsplänen und Studienaufträgen, in Vitrinen und auf Sockeln in Ausstellungshallen. Und in weiteren Gedankensträngen, deren Netz von Assoziationen und Querverbindungen so eng wurde, dass noch viel mehr Ideen darin hängen blieben. Hier würde ein Zitat zum Rhizom, wie Deleuze und Guattari es beschrieben, passen. Oder aus einem der anderen Bücher, die auf den Zeichentischen liegen bleiben.

Pensée Sauvage

Die Modelle

Ebenfalls würde ein Satz über Modellierungen passen, wie Hans-Jörg Rheinberger sie beschrieb: Das Setting limitiert die möglichen Resultate eines Versuchs, jeder Test testet in erster Linie die Versuchsanordnung. Es gibt Holz-, Stein- und Metallmodelle im Büro, in allen Grössen. Einige sind schwer in der Hand, andere leicht anzuheben. Anders als vor dreissig Jahren können nun im Computermodell auch Rundumbewegungen im Raum erprobt werden, doch es gibt immer noch unzählige Modelle in den Kisten, auf den Kisten, auf den Arbeitstischen, über den Büchergestellen.

Into the Book

«Über den Tellerrand schauen», sogar «querdenken» gibt das Wörterbuch als Übersetzung von «out of the box» an. Am häufigsten aber übersetzt der Online-Translator: «out of the box». Der Ausdruck ist längst in allen Sprachen angekommen und auch auf diesem Buch-Kaleidoskop, in dem sich Elemente der Architektur von agps zu einem Panorama unendlicher Möglichkeiten vervielfachen.

Capturing Thoughts

Sometimes I will jot down thoughts to capture them. Only concrete logic can do justice to a savage mind—at least that's what Claude Lévi-Strauss, who reinvented the discipline of ethnology, advised in 1962. Architecture isn't lacking in terms of the concrete: each line, each word, each surface relates to a concrete object. Architects think about bolt heads and regional plans, art and technology, science and everyday life. There exist many connections between these areas, sometimes countless it seems.

Out of the box

agps are many, and they are everywhere. Look for them in Zurich, and you'll be connected with Los Angeles—or Santa Ynez or Barcelona. And their thoughts, likewise, tend to be in many places at once.

"Out of the Box," written on the cover of their kaleidoscopic picture book, contains literal as well as figurative meanings: the box refers to the archive in which models, drawings, and data are protected from dust and cyber-attacks. But the box also represents the norm from which the architects have liberated themselves again and again.

Playbook

Actually, the box is bursting at the seams. The material is angular, flighty, too big, too bulky, it overflows, dissipates. It's nearly impossible to compress. And yet, when I was an intern at agps in the 90s, we made an attempt at introducing an order. On hundreds of small slips of paper, we wrote down the script for their first office presentations in Zurich, nearly thirty years ago in Fritz Schwarz's architecture forum at Neumarkt—the Kellertheater.

Invitations

"Open structures"—that's what the six architects of agps used as a title back then. Later these work presentations were often named after the projects: simple and to the point. And what they showed again and again was an openness of mind and the liberty to freely associate. When invited to speak, they often talked about "heterogenous productions" and "topolectic drawing," but also—as the decades went on—about tango, root networks, *cadavres exquis*, utopias, and millennium models.

Blurring

We didn't write a lecture though, we wrote a script. By using this format, we hoped to retain our freedom to think wildly and associatively. There were more than two hundred notes, more than two hundred slides, and far more than two hundred ideas, which we then used to enchant—or rather: stun—the audience on the cool stone steps of the basement at Neumarkt. I can still hear the rapid clicking, a runaway rhythm that with its tempo created a kind of blurring effect, defying all conventional rules of elocution.

Pensée Sauvage

Motion

Rules, however, were of acute interest to us. We read Umberto Eco and thought about the chaos of relations in which new rules are formed: rules we perhaps didn't know about yet. Rules in motion for an artwork in motion. This would offer the opportunity for a multitude of personal interventions, as we learned from the pope of Semiotics, Umberto Eco (*The Open Work*, 1962).

Pensée sauvage—The Savage Mind

These texts from the time of intellectual departure in the postwar period resonated with us. We became adepts of wild thinking, and what we associated with it probably surpassed anything that Lévi-Strauss had ever presumed of his readers. We folded roofs and creased facades and allowed the topography of the landscape to reverberate in the buildings.

Wild Thoughts

On one of Lévi-Strauss' book covers (*La pensée sauvage*, 1962), we can see a *pensée* (also called *fleur de pense* or *viola tricolor*), a wild pansy. He uses it to demonstrate his hypothesis of concrete logic. As evidenced by different ethnographic texts, it is possible to deduce the parentage of a plant simply by looking at its petals: wild thoughts and wild plants are organized according to a specific set of rules.

Pain Relief

Understanding wilderness: the wild pansy can be used to treat inflammation and pain, while its cultivated counterparts lack such medicinal properties. Thoughts, likewise, should remain wild, moving, open, inspired, improvised, and be free to come to us from any direction.

Different Readings

Letting go, grasping, sounding out the interstitial spaces. Perhaps they have long since been condensed, amalgamated, who doesn't read between the lines after all? Now that we've determined the order of the illustrations, who is still free to play? Our thoughts are free, and they combine with other fragments. Interwoven conjunctions becoming entire networks.

A Rhizome

"Open Structures," like later lectures, exhibitions, projects, was a fireworks of images and words, fragments of architectural ideas, many of which were never built, but rather made their way as thought experiments. They would show up in competition plans and study contracts, in the display cases and on the pedestals of exhibition halls, and in ensuing trains of thought whose net of associations and interrelations has been so finely woven that ever more ideas are caught in it. A quote on the rhizome, as Deleuze and Guattari defined it, would be fitting here. Or one from any of the other books that remain on the drawing tables.

Pensée Sauvage

The Models

Likewise, we could quote a passage on testing as Hans-Jörg Rheinberger described it: The setting delimitates the number of possible results of any attempt; each test, first and foremost, tests the experimental setup. There are wood, stone, and metal models in all shapes and sizes in the office. Some weigh heavy in our hands, others are light and easily picked up. Unlike thirty years ago, today we are able to test entire rotational movements in a space by using computer modelling. And yet, there are still countless models in boxes, on boxes, on tables, up high on the shelves.

Into the book

To "think outside the box," or in this case "out of the box," is a common English idiom that has made its way into the vocabulary of various languages around the world as well as into this book kaleidoscope in which elements of agps' architecture multiply into a panorama of endless possibilities.

Hovering

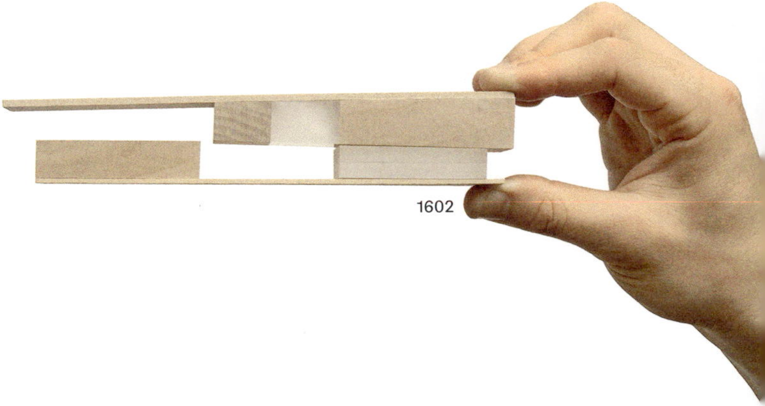

1602

Hovering

redbox
CARENINI HOME

9801

Hovering

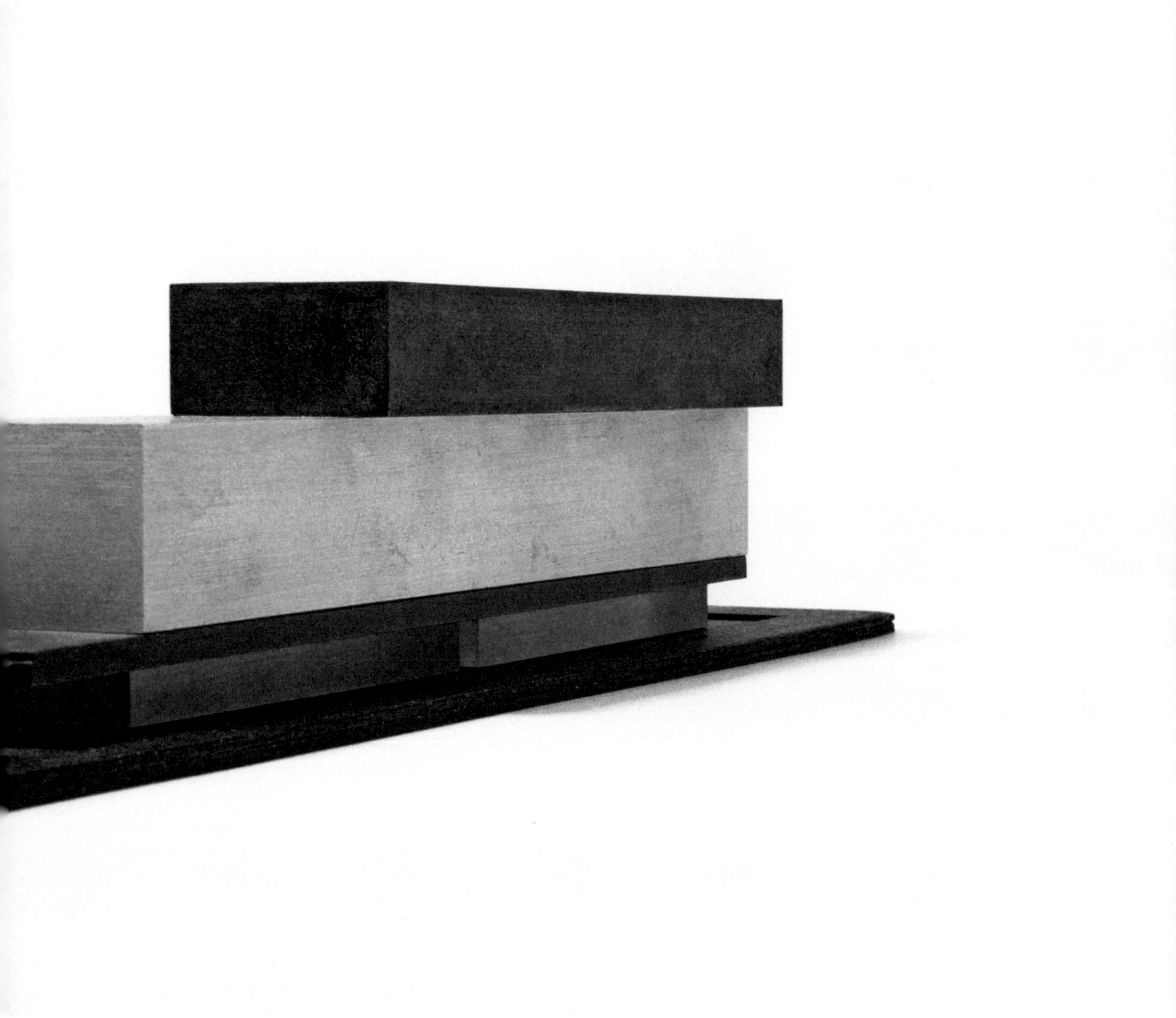

0201

0201

Hovering

Hovering

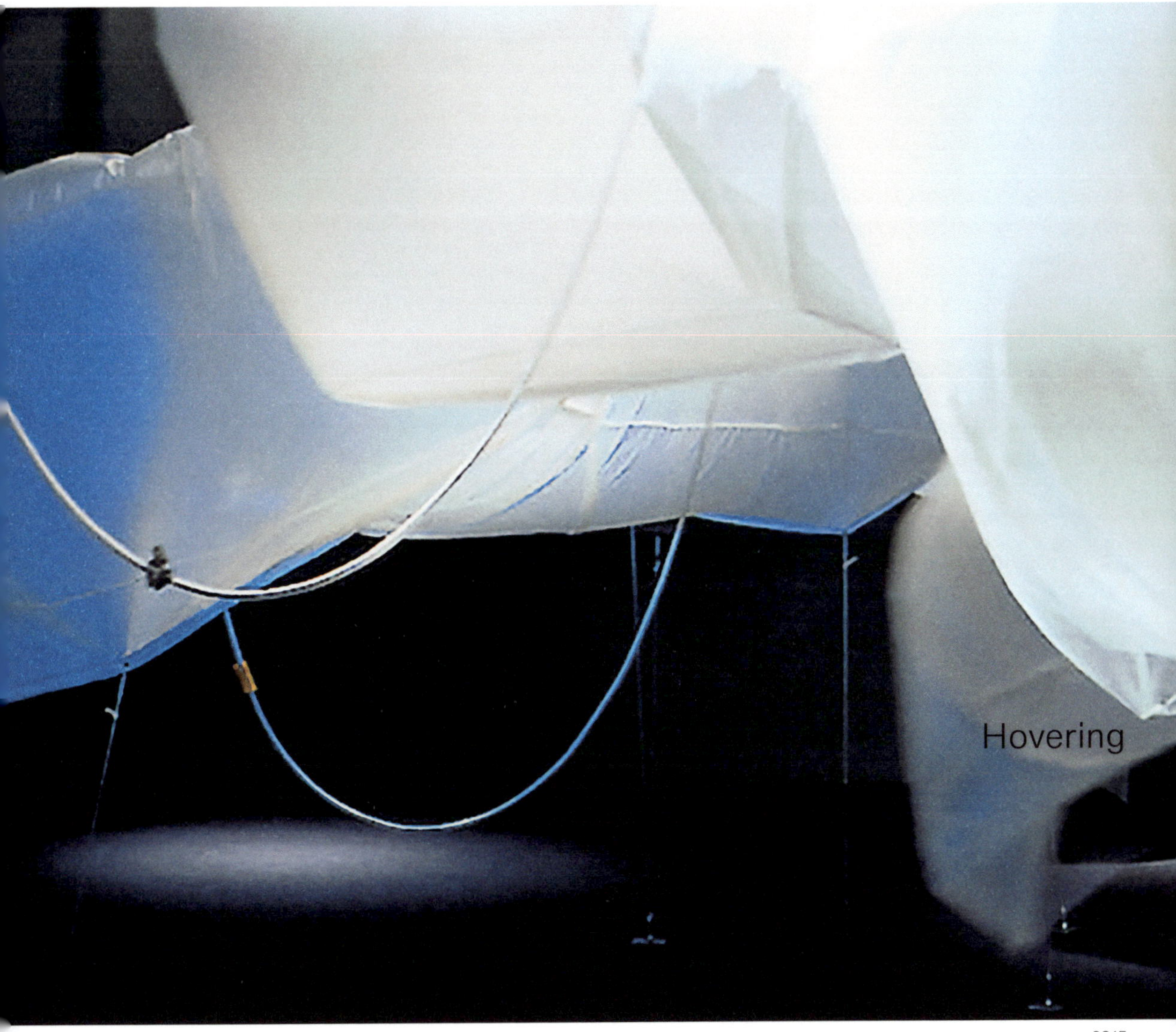

Hovering

0104

Hovering

1615

Hovering

Hovering

0402

Hovering

Hovering

1811

Hovering

0613

Hovering

Blurred

Blurred

Blurred

0902

Blurred

Blurred

9701

Blurred

0902

Blurred

Blurred

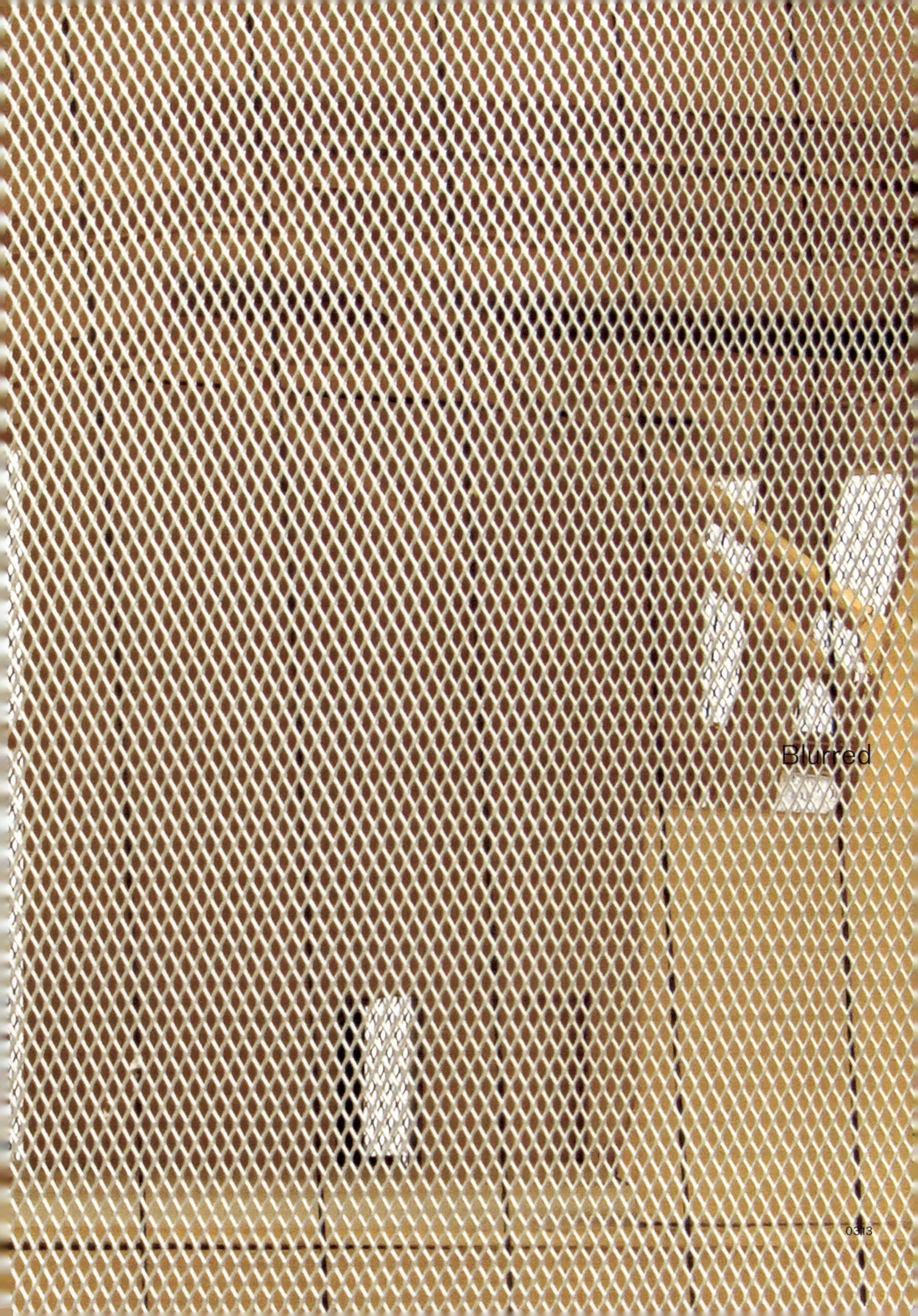

Blurred

03.13

Blurred

1407

Blurred

Sequential

0201

Sequential

0902

0902

Sequential

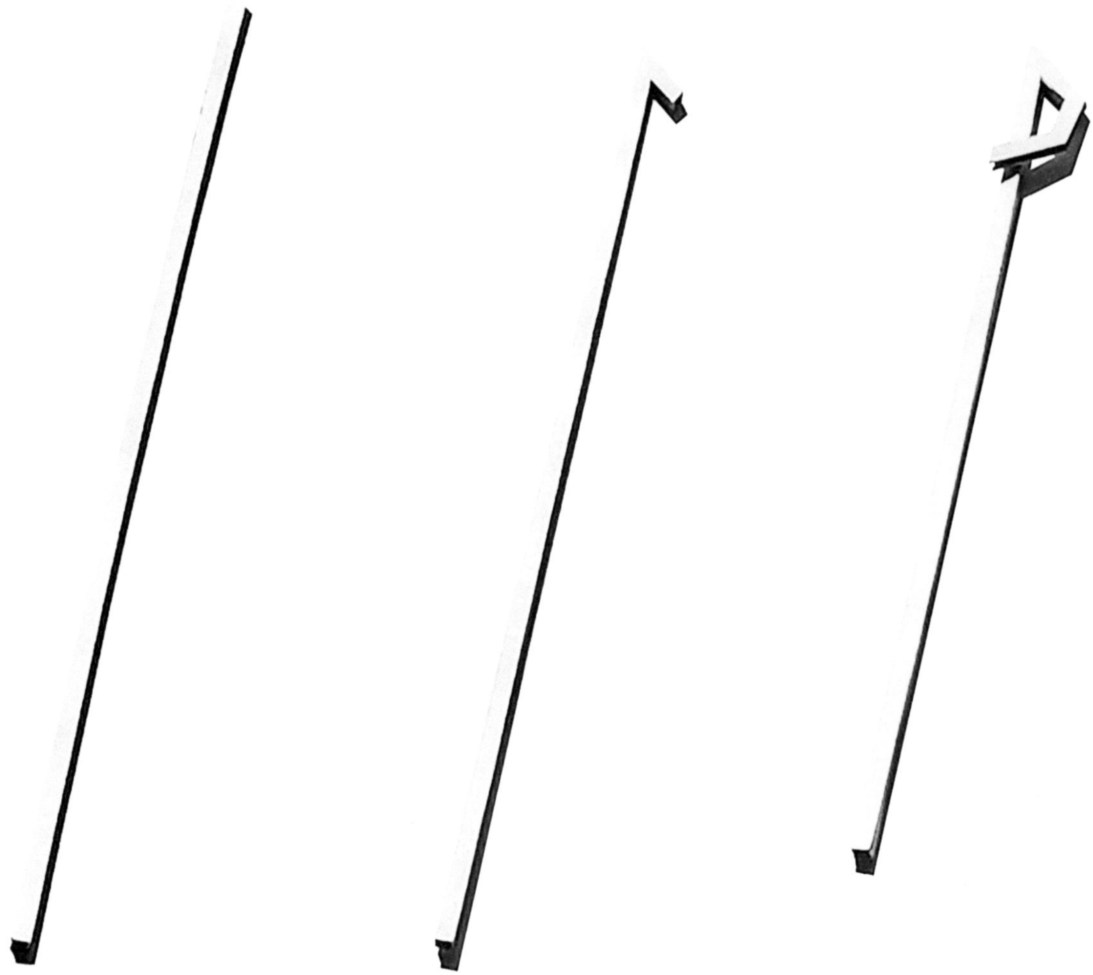

0312

Sequential

Sequential

Sequential

9403

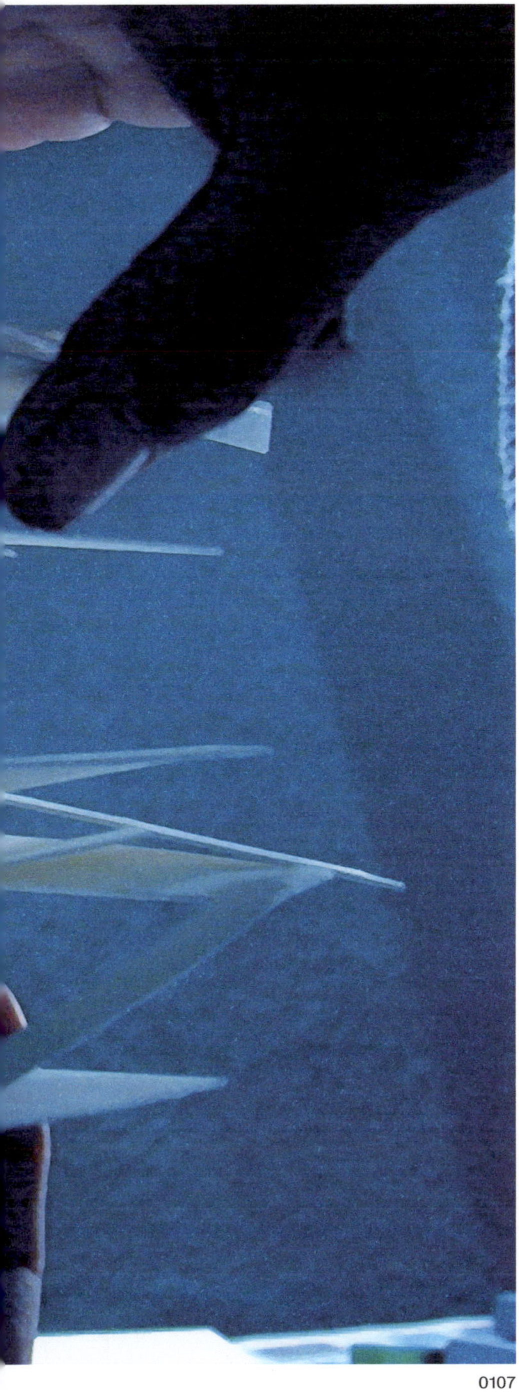

Sequential

0402

Sequential

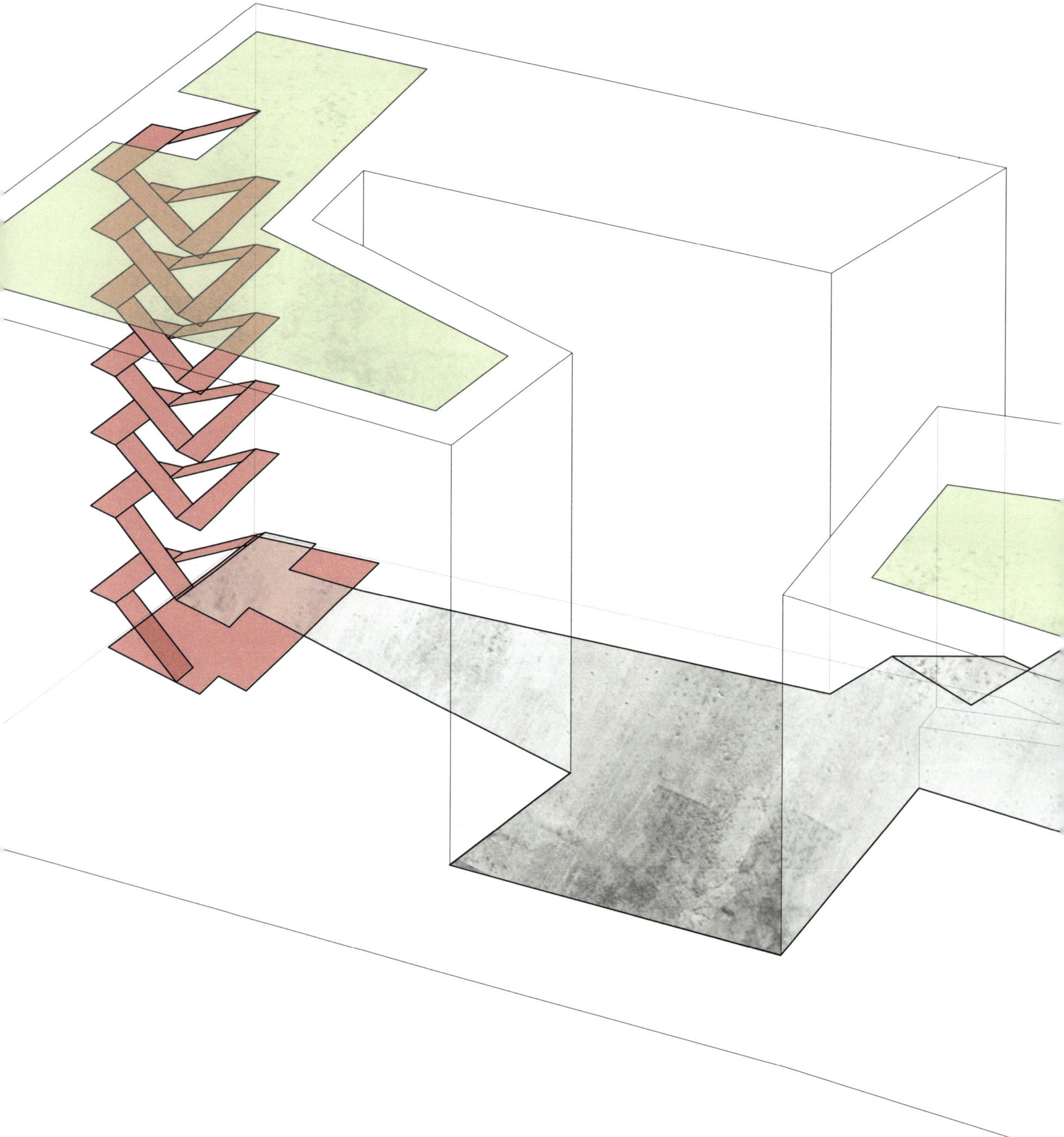

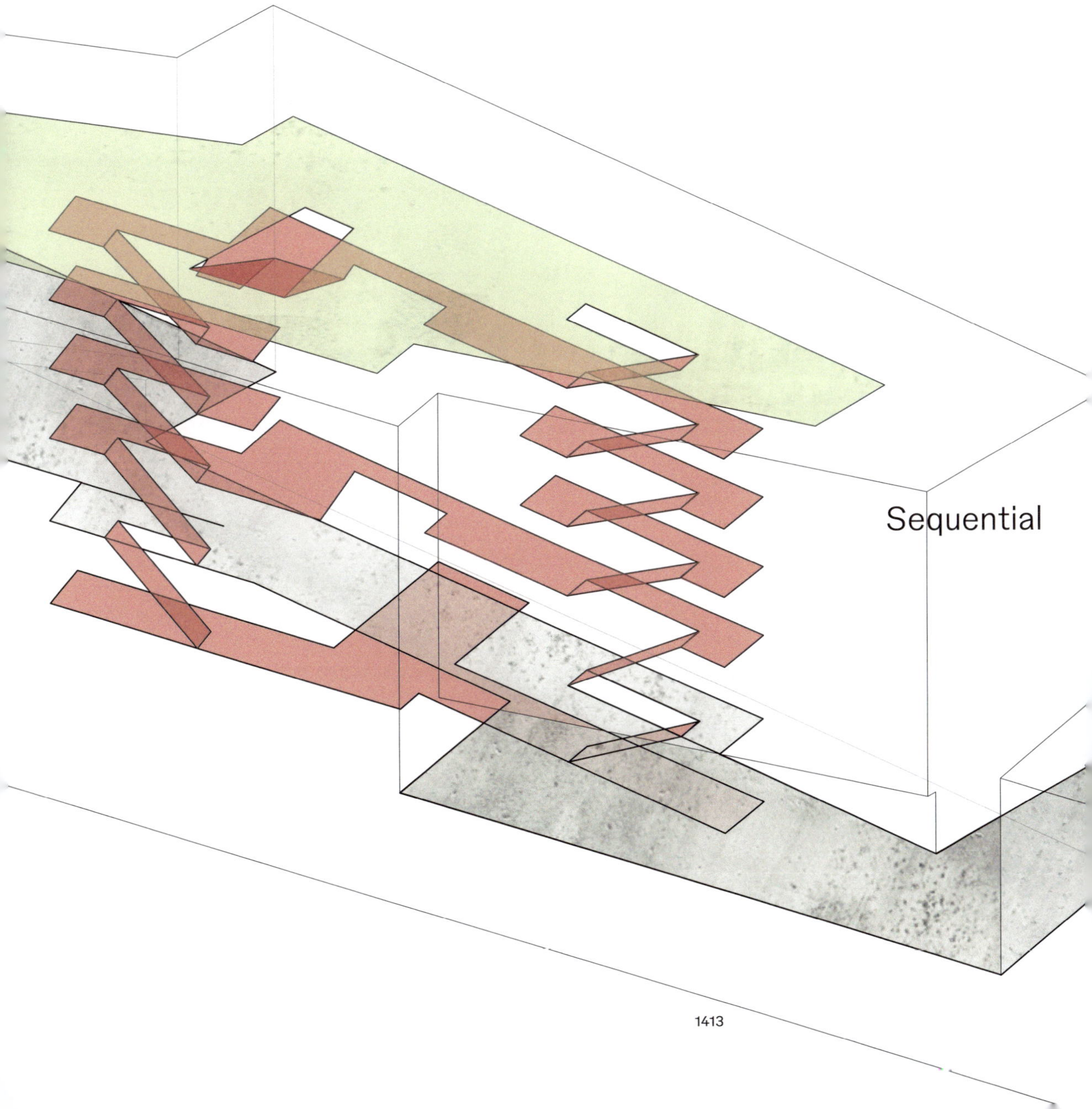
Sequential

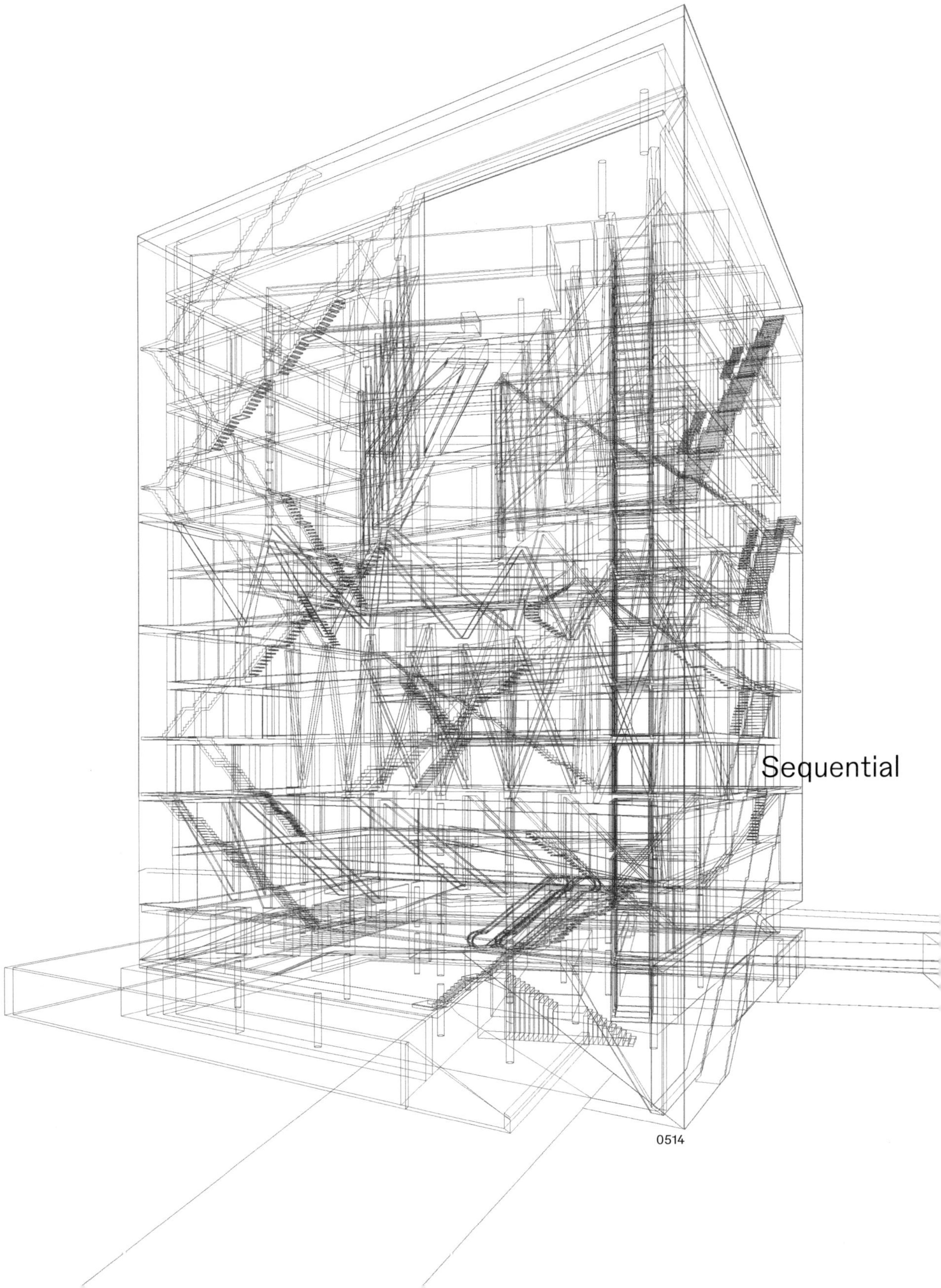

Sequential

0514

Void

Void

Void

0810

Void

9402

Void

1415

Void

0629

Void

1409

Void

Void

1717

0303

Void

Void

0301

0402

Void

9701

Void

Sculpted

9404

Sculpted

Sculpted

0608

Sculpted

Sculpted

0916

Sculpted

Sculpted

0402

Sculpted

0608

9201

Sculpted

Sculpted

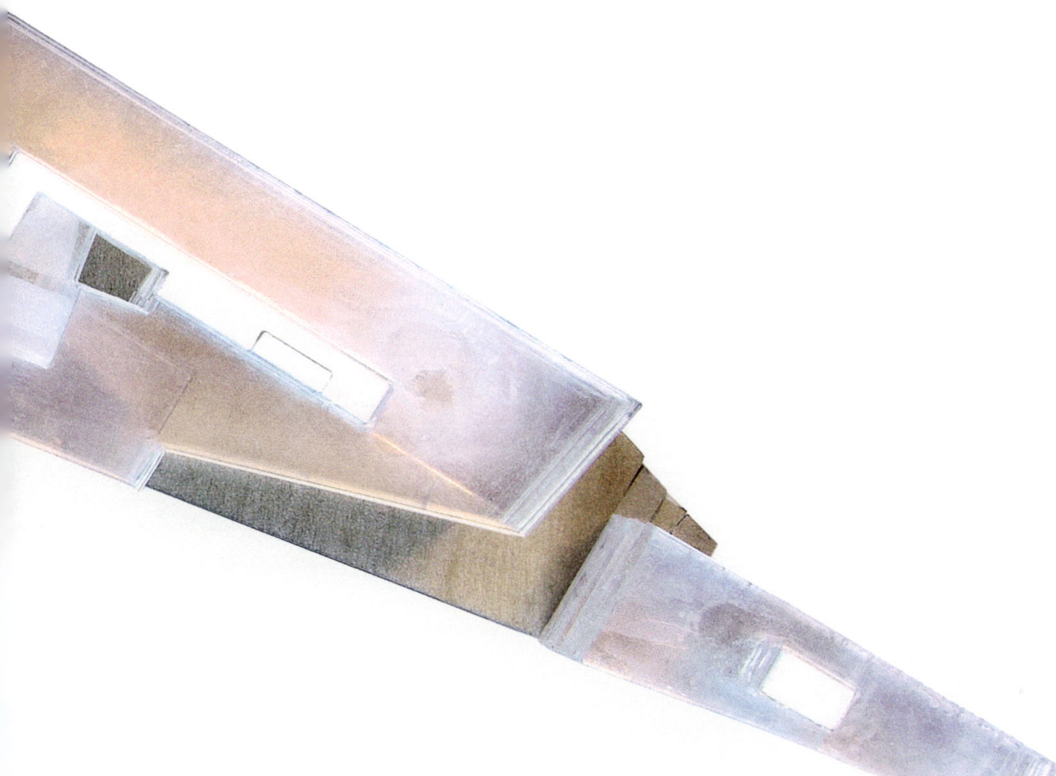

Sculpted

0620

Sculpted

Sculpted

1515

Sculpted

Project list

9001 Lunch Shelters, Los Angeles, US | p. 114

9102 Hollywood House, Los Angeles, US | pp. 30, 35, 112, 122
9103 Topanga House, Los Angeles, US | p. 104

9201 Esslinger Dreieck Areal, Esslingen, CH | p. 274
9202 Esslingen Forchbahn, Esslingen, CH | p. 108
9204 Esslingen Post, Esslingen, CH | p. 102
9206 Koreatown Storefronts, Los Angeles, US | p. 54

9402 Berufsschule Schützenareal, Zürich, CH | pp. 76, 238
9403 Zahnarztpraxis Geiser und Kleiser, Zürich, CH | pp. 136, 221
9404 Hillside Housing, Tokyo, JP | p. 258

9505 Photovoltaic Installations, Los Angeles, US | p. 116

9701 Dock E Flughafen Zürich, Zürich, CH | pp. 52, 90, 98, 107, 197, 255

9801 Waschanstalt Wollishofen, Zürich, CH | pp. 32, 162
9803 Esslingen Dorfladen I, Esslingen, CH | p. 174

9901 Geschäftshäuser Swing, Wallisellen, CH | p. 17
9903 Ur Fenil, Origlio, CH | pp. 50, 110

0101 Wohnung Semmler, Kilchberg, CH | p. 124
0104 Merbag Areal, Zürich, CH | pp. 74, 170
0107 Mercedes-Benz Museum, Stuttgart, DE | p. 222
0114 Children's Museum, Los Angeles, US | p. 66

0201 Stellwerk, Winterthur, CH | pp. 164, 165, 212
0205 Hohenbühl, Zürich, CH | p. 127, 188
0215 Latent Utopias at Steirischer Herbst, Graz, AT | pp. 10, 160, 168, 282, 284, 285

0301 Hohenrain, Kilchberg, CH | pp. 125, 134, 208, 251
0302 Restaurant Flickflauder, Weissbad, CH | pp. 41, 43, 271
0303 Integra Office, Wallisellen, CH | pp. 24, 248
0308 Theater Stadthof 11, Zürich, CH | p. 64
0312 Nam June Paik Museum, Seoul, SK | pp. 216, 218
0313 Portland Aerial Tram, Portland, US | pp. 12, 14, 204

0402 Nanjing International Planning Center, Nanjing, CN | pp. 79, 176, 190, 225, 252, 272
0403 adidas Football Facility, Herzogenaurach, DE | p. 142
0405 Zurich International School, Adliswil, CH | pp. 46, 88
0406 Einhausung Schwamendingen, Zürich, CH | pp. 87, 90
0409 Polizei- und Justizzentrum, Zürich, CH | p. 20
0411 adidas Brand Center, Herzogenaurach, DE | pp. 138, 139
0414 Topanga Ranch, Los Angeles, US | pp. 22, 36

0501 Wolfratshauserstrasse, München, DE | p. 194
0514 Universitäts- und Landesbibliothek, Darmstadt, DE | pp. 33, 229

0601 Integra H2/4, Wallisellen, CH | pp. 53, 202
0602 Integra i37, Wallisellen, CH | p. 49
0605 Haidenauplatz, München, DE | p. 90
0608 Kesslerstrasse, Zollikon, CH | pp. 262, 264, 266, 273
0611 Bioforce, Roggwil, CH | p. 121

Marc Angélil studied architecture at ETH Zürich, where he also completed his doctoral dissertation. He has taught at Harvard University, University of Southern California, and as Professor at ETH Zürich he conducted research on social and spatial developments of metropolitan regions worldwide from 1994 to 2019. He held the Kenzo Tange Visiting Professorship in Architecture and Urban Planning and Design in 2021. He is a fellow of the Bund Schweizer Architekten (BSA) and was a board member of the Holcim Foundation for Sustainable Construction from 1993 to 2020. Marc Angélil has been a partner at agps since 1982.

Sarah Graham holds a Bachelor of Arts in Art History and Design from Stanford University and a Master of Architecture from Harvard University. She has been adjunct professor at the University of Southern California and visiting professor at the Rhode Island School of Design, Harvard Graduate School of Design, University of California Berkeley, and Nanjing University. She is a member of the Bund Schweizer Architekten (BSA) and a Fellow of the American Institute of Architects (FAIA). She was on the Alumni Board of the Harvard Graduate School of Design from 2012 to 2016. Sarah Graham has been a partner at agps since 1982 and leads the Los Angeles office.

Manuel Scholl studied architecture at ETH Zürich. He worked as an architect in Ticino, USA, and Spain, taught and researched at ETH Zürich and was Tenure Professor for Urban Design at the Leibniz University Hannover from 2009 until 2014. Manuel Scholl is a fellow of the Bund Schweizer Architekten (BSA), is board member of the Ernst-Schindler-Foundation, and member of the Gestaltungsbeirat to the city of Wolfsburg. Additionally, he is internationally active as a juror and expert for urban and architectural projects. Manuel Scholl has been a partner at agps since 1992 and leads the Zürich office.

agps architecture is a design team with studios in Zurich and Los Angeles, bridging the domains of urban design, infrastructure, landscape, and architecture. The group considers architecture a collaborative enterprise, investigating relationships between design processes and the built environment. From the development of urban strategies to the exploration of construction techniques, the work engages in a search for the yet undiscovered; conceptual, multilayered, and succinct approaches to architecture are explored.

Text

Sabine von Fischer is an architectural historian, architect, and writer. She studied architecture at ETH Zürich, where she also completed her doctoral dissertation. She taught and researched at ETH Zürich, the Canadian Center for Architecture in Montréal, the Swiss Federal Institute of Technology Lausanne, the Zürich University of the Arts, and the Max-Planck-Institute for the History of Science Berlin. Sabine von Fischer has published several books and periodicals and was in charge of the *Neue Zürcher Zeitung* architecture and design section from 2019 to 2022.

Photo credits

Michael Arden | p. 112
Ralph Bensberg | pp. 52, 107, 128, 197
Arge Zayetta | pp. 89/90 (9701), 98
Alain Bucher, Holcim Foundation | p. 184
Brigida González | pp. 192, 198, 214 right
Andrea Helbling, Arazebra | pp. 30, 35, 40, 41, 188
Gaston Wicky | p. 162
Eduard Hueber, archphoto | pp. 54, 104, 108, 114 left
Reinhard Zimmermann | pp. 24, 46, 49, 53, 124, 136, 140, 165, 174, 202, 221, 248, 264, 266
Eric Staudenmaier Photography | pp. 36, 38, 39, 200

Architectural art cooperation

0205 facade design in cooperation with Blanca Blarer

p. 188

0303 elevator with plants, Blanca Blarer

p. 248

0902 facade design and signage in cooperation with Marco Ganz

pp. 192, 198

1215 color design, Marco Ganz

p. 34

Further information on www.agps.ch

Imprint

Book concept
Manuel Scholl, Marc Angélil, Frederick Kim, agps architecture

Book design and editorial work
Manuel Scholl, Lina von Waldkirch, agps architecture

Graphic design
Sibylle Brodbeck and Schön & Berger, Zürich

Typography
Peclet, TIGHTYPE, Germany

Translation and Proof reading
Lisa Schons

Printing and binding
DZA Druckerei zu Altenburg GmbH, Altenburg

Park Books AG
Niederdorfstrasse 54
8001 Zurich
Switzerland
www.park-books.com

Park Books is being supported by the Federal Office of Culture with a general subsidy for the years 2021–2024.

ISBN 978-3-03860-264-4